Sing

"Sometimes an anthology will remind us of just how much the poet as editor can bring to the conception and execution of a work, turning it from a mere compilation of random poems into a wonderfully conceived and eloquently expressed grand poem of multiple voices that is marked by all the qualities we want in the best poems: passion, risk, daring, grace, imagination, urgency, compassion, visionary power, and profound homage to the grounding of tradition. In what can only be called a historical anthology of Indigenous poets from the Americas, Allison Hedge Coke has given us a stunning gift that is splendid because of the brilliance of the individual and eclectic poems collected, and richer for the coherent collective song that the anthology represents. This is a big, fat book of endless pleasures that helps us to re-imagine America!"

—Kwame Dawes, editor of *Red: Contemporary Black British Poetry*

"*Sing* . . . es como un ánfora de plumas colocada sobre las cumbres de una expresión tanto oral como literaria que representada en varios idiomas— originarios o modernos—convoca a un ánima sola, hechizándonos con esa sensibilidad sobre la que se han construido un carácter, una identidad y una voluntad de belleza presente en cada gesto de afirmación y resistencia ante sus más antiguos y fieros depredadores. En manos de la poeta Allison Hedge Coke, aquí palpita el canto, la música y la mejor poesía de los pueblos indígenas de las Américas."

—Nancy Morejón, Cuban poet laureate

"In celebration and triumph, *Sing* raises its riveting collective voice to the rafters. This is the soundtrack of a new world birthed of tales firmly rooted to the earth and sky; this is the soundtrack of lives as we must learn to live them."

—Patricia Smith, author of *Blood Dazzler*

"I will sing this book to my children. I will give this book to my cadre, the ones that dreamt it in the sixties when they journeyed thousands of miles in search of it. Hedge Coke calls us to the new cycle of Indigenous poetry of the Americas. A monumental triumph."

—Juan Felipe Herrera, author of *Half of the World in Light: New and Selected Poems*

"From Canada to Chile (and Colombia, Mexico, Guatemala, the United States, Ecuador, Venezuela, and Peru) in English, Spanish, Quechua, Wayuu, Mapuche, Comanche, and more, the range of voices represented here is astounding. *Sing* celebrates the life and breadth of Indigenous American poetry. This long-awaited anthology is a beautiful and necessary treasure."

—Camille T. Dungy, editor of *Black Nature: Four Centuries of African American Nature Poetry*

"*Sing: Poetry from the Indigenous Americas* showcases writing of American Indian poets from north to south in the Western Hemisphere, giving readers a rare and direct connection into the complexity of their lives and thinking today."

—Carla Blank, co-editor of *Pow Wow: Charting the Fault Lines in the American Experience—Short Fiction from Then to Now*

"One of the most essential anthologies of recent years, *Sing* is rare in scope and insight. The poems found here are a testament to the power of indigeneity and the urgency of our current moment. This book sings the hemisphere into glorious fullness, teaching us the connections between us, and the great schisms between our knowledge and our actions."

—Matthew Shenoda, author of *Seasons of Lotus, Seasons of Bone*

"Panoramic, wise, and palpable texts of beauty and vitality. This is what the world needs to wake itself up to its own better self and imagination."

—Anne Waldman, author of *Manatee/Humanity*

Volume 68

Sun Tracks
An American Indian Literary Series

Series Editor
Ofelia Zepeda

Editorial Committee
Larry Evers
Joy Harjo
Geary Hobson
N. Scott Momaday
Irvin Morris
Simon J. Ortiz
Kate Shanley
Leslie Marmon Silko
Luci Tapahonso

Sing

Poetry from the Indigenous Americas

EDITED BY Allison Adelle Hedge Coke

ASSOCIATE EDITORS: Travis Brent Hedge Coke,
Eric Wayne Dickey, and Joseph Ohmann-Krause

The University of Arizona Press   Tucson

The University of Arizona Press
© 2011 Allison Hedge Coke and Poetry Enterprises

www.uapress.arizona.edu

Library of Congress Cataloging-in-Publication Data
Sing : poetry from the indigenous Americas / edited by Allison Adelle Hedge Coke.
     p. cm. — (Sun tracks ; v. 68)
  Includes poems and translations or versions thereof, in the Fall 2006/Winter 2007
edition of Topos : poetry International, under the title Ahani : indigenous American poetry,
edited by Allison Adelle Hedge Coke.
    ISBN 978-0-8165-2891-2 (pbk. : alk. paper) 1. American poetry—Indian authors.
2. Indian poetry—Translations into English. 3. Indians—Poetry. I. Coke, Allison Hedge.
II. Title: Poetry from the indigenous Americas.
   PS591.I55S55 2011
   811'.6080897—dc23

                        2011018310

Publication of this book is made possible in part by the proceeds of a permanent
endowment created with the assistance of a Challenge Grant from the National
Endowment for the Humanities, a federal agency.

Manufactured in the United States of America on acid-free, archival-quality paper
containing a minimum of 30% post-consumer waste and processed chlorine free.

16   15   14   13   12   6   5   4   3   2

Contents

✦ ÑEÑE'I HA-ṢA:GID (IN THE MIDST OF SONGS)

✦ SOBRE LOS CAMPOS (THROUGH THE FIELDS)

✦ **THE LIST WE MAKE**

Acknowledgments

Sing: Indigenous Poetry of the Americas pays tribute to the millions of remarkable people descending from antediluvian inhabitants of the Western Hemisphere. The editor thanks each and every contributor and those poets willing to contribute poems that page restriction prohibited inclusion of. The editor extends great gratitude to the translators who worked to bring exceptional original poetry to publication herein, with special thanks to Cristina Eisenberg, Juan Felipe Herrera, and Laura Ortega. To John Damon for his assistance with Tohono O'odham linguistics and diacriticals. To Ofelia Zepeda, Patti Hartmann, and Sherwin Bitsui for championing the work. To James Thomas Stevens for his patience and, through the invitation of Mary Lawlor and Muhlenberg College, provides a venue at the United Nations for included poets to annually speak. To Travis Hedge Coke for editorial assistance on this volume.

Special thanks goes to Eric Dickey for his exceptional vision, magnanimity, and tireless, pro bono work toward this provable end, and to Joseph Krause for generous support in this imperative cultural literary event. To serendipity for the timing of the invitation to guest-edit *To Topos: Poetry International*, which came while the editor was a first-time participating poet at the International Festival of Poetry in Medellín. To Sherwin, for obtaining the initial invitation for participation in Medellín and to all the organizing host officials and poets in international and world festivals in Venezuela, Argentina, Colombia, the States, and Canada, for subsequent invitations, making this compilation work possible. Special thanks to Fernando Rendon, Gloria Chvatal, and Prometeo for building a platform for international Indigenous poets to convene. To Hugo Jamioy Juagibioy, Ariruma Kowii, and Aty Jeney for inviting participation in Colombia and requesting we offer their poetry in testimony of Indigenous Colombian and Ecuadorian experience and their request that the editor find a way to unify the poets, the voices, of the North and South, Eagle and Condor. To Ariruma and Hugo for conceiving our gathering.

To Al Hunter, Quincy Troupe, Roberta Hill, Simon Ortiz, Joy Harjo, Arthur Sze, Sam Hamill, Jack Hirschman, Jayne Cortez, and Rita Dove for participating in the festivals and influencing this work. To Joy Harjo and Sherwin Bitsui for suggesting the University of Arizona Press as host publisher for the culminating anthology presented here. To the press for publishing this work. To Sherwin, Hugo, Fredy, Joy, Gregorio, Natalia, Jessie, and Lindantonella for shared declaration of Indigenous poets in Medellín, 2007.

To Ramon Palomares for every dog wagging campo poem.

To R. L. Hedge Coke for breadth, clarity, culture, inclusivity, patience, and song.

To the Warao poets in the Delta Orinoco, Tucupita, and to Miguel in Maturín.

To Hazel Mellow Walter Hedgecoke for strength, patience, and wisdom.

To LeAnne Howe for the light.

To Wang Ping for the canoe.

To Poetry.

To Life.

In Memoriam—

Special tribute to Jack Forbes and John Damon, who both crossed over during the making of this book. May we remember them both.

Special thanks to the Lannan Foundation and the Weymouth Center for support of the editorial work in generous residencies.

Sing

Introduction

In blood, in pulse, and just as driving as any homing device we bear, movement, travel, journey proves imperative; we come and go, come and go, always seeking what we do not know, have not seen, some of us always returning, to reveal the witnessings and to revel in the familiar. Sometimes, in the movement, motion, cadence, rhythm, lyric, song appears, as if music just existed for us to collide into, and maybe it does. In movement, songs reveal what approaches need be made to sustain and continue. Notes of the everyday push/pull us to where we need be in some harmonic luxury. It is a soulful thing. Perhaps we've never been without song, or the ability to sing it. Sometimes songs present themselves in the most unfamiliar moments, improvisationally. Sometimes songs connect, familiarize. Sometimes the orchestration of tones, or words, heals. Sometimes we actually learn to let go and let them lead us. Sometimes we follow to sing.

In 2004, after the publication of *Rock, Ghost, Willow, Deer,* and some earlier successes, including *Dog Road Woman,* I was offered a National Endowment for the Humanities Distinguished Visiting Professorship at Hartwick College in Oneonta, New York. I was surprised at the offer. I'd just returned from directing a World Poetry Bout in Billings, at the High Plains Book Festival, in which I organized and hosted the initial All-Indian Bout (sanctioned by the Taos Poetry Circus), the Joe Hipp Tribute, and was expecting to continue my work in Sioux Falls, South Dakota. In recent years, I'd dedicated myself to building community and teaching dignity through the arts, propagating South Dakotan and regional literary activity and opening youth arts venues, while consistently lobbying for preservation of an Indigenous city of mounded earthworks that had been nearly erased just past the time the buffalo were nearly exterminated. Both intentionally. While I lived in my little hundred-year-old turquoise brick house just east of the Falls of the Big Sioux River, the ruins of a city of ten thousand original people, ten or fifteen minutes farther east and also on the river, was a constant consideration of mine. It was a city among cities in the world in the early 1700s, ten thousand citizens in the main metropolis area and outlying settlements spread over hundreds and hundreds of acres in what now exists as eastern South Dakota and western Iowa. There was nothing at all in the local curriculum about the site, though some of the builders' descendents were within driving distance, and very little information was available from the neighboring state of Iowa, which had acquired and was attempting to protect that side of the greater site. I'd begun research with Iowan officials, Adrien Hannus at Augustana, the state archaeologists in South Dakota, private owners of the some of the property, and members of the originating nations of this place. European-descent specialists called the builders Oneota.

As a poet, I tend to be impressed with duality and kinship in language. I have a greater inclination to focus on language, on kinship and pattern, than I do on my personal achievement. It is only because I was there that I could put myself into the explication of a moment, of a scenario. Had the call come from a college in any other town than Oneonta, perhaps I would have stayed where I was, declining the offer. Though I relished the opportunity, going, as I did, from 750 students to 35, a significant change, provided an avenue for personal measure, or primary revelation in critical awareness of significant and substantial immediate loss in mass destruction of hundreds of monumental earthworks, marking thousands of lives cradled in the two cities I temporarily left behind, Blood Run and Sioux Falls. Climbing into the car to make the trek, the consideration and motion propelled me to song early on. It was my drive and company throughout the journey. I knew no other way.

When I reached a place with Iroquoian-Huron lingual trace, Sandusky ("Cold Water"), I went over to Erie to sing a bit of thanks there, to remember my familial kinship in the region. On my lakeside walk, an elderly woman motioned me to sit by her on a bench. She began telling me how the water was when she was young, how they'd skate on it frozen over, and how the lakes don't freeze over anymore. How people could cross the lake, at one time, on foot. I felt her sadness and concern and recalled huge drifts of snow and thick, thick ice I haven't witnessed much since my youth. The world was changing. Yet the story of ice was still here, the story of crossing, and tapped personally by childhood stories of my grandmas coming down through the waters, from Quebec and Ontario to Ohio and to Michigan, then Illinois, and eventually to Indian Territory, where one met my grandfather (from mounds ancestry in the Southeast) and the two of them united. I remembered stories of rib bones strapped to moccasin soles to skate a lake's long distance and held the memory of that ascendant pair speaking over ten languages each, *just to get by in those years,* stories close to my own wanderlust and love for beauty and drive for knowledge wherever it may be. I wondered if Granny had been in this same place herself.

I'd slowed, come to a travel rest, in Sioux Falls due to Blood Run. I couldn't leave without working fully to correct a historical and contemporary crime—cultural erasure. Couldn't move forward until the lobbying culminated in a success story—acknowledgment, preservation, protection— especially since I had grandchildren born in Sioux Falls. When, at a hearing in Oacoma, after years of working to convince the state to free the land from the hundred-year settler descendents, and would-be developers, still tilling and graveling graves and sometimes still looting them, this solo civilian testimony, backed with letters from my students and hard facts, went from factual lecture to a pouring out of persona poems composed at the site. This moved the Game, Fish, and Parks officials to a change of heart and led to an unprecedented unanimous vote to secure and preserve the historical site.

Soon afterward, I began to collect these poems into a manuscript while simultaneously finalizing a volume of contemporary labor poems, including building and growing poems, from my work with Inland Construction and sharecropping tobacco in my North Carolina days. The two volumes wholly played upon each other in my consciousness—traditional work and contemporary work, time upon time, shifting with eras' transforming need. The work was peppered with both people of peace and villains: people building places to live and revere, growing food and sustaining themselves, then finding themselves infiltrated, and now the evidence of their labors nearly erased—intentionally. It maddened me.

In Oneonta, I invited James Thomas Stevens, a terrifically talented and intelligent Mohawk poet, to serve as visiting writer in my classes. While he was in residence, we were both shown the original treaty between Mohawk people and the queen on behalf of Hartwick, the school's namesake, and told the story of Hartwick's plan to create something of a pluralistic utopia. His partner (James Fenimore Cooper's grandfather), while the hopeful Hartwick was abroad looking for *good (white) people* to populate the parcel, swindled Hartwick and sold the land off to anyone with money, in a longhouse land, where the fiery Clinton campaign later ravaged Iroquoia under Washington's directives, in his attempt to exterminate the original people of the region to expand the ideology, resources, and wealth of the British colonies, despite the fact that their motherlands were not in favor of the expansion at that time and that the *patriots* were breaking all code of conduct, including treaties, in doing so. Despite the hard history, I loved the Oneonta area (from *Onaanta,* "mountain," "sloped outcropping of rocks," place where there is an outcropping of rock, so like Oneota, "people who sprang from an outcropping of rock"), the Catskills somewhat akin to my sloping Appalachian youth—such a beautiful place, so lived in.

My tenure in New York ended when I began work at Northern Michigan University in Marquette on Lake Superior. *Off Season City Pipe,* my labor poetry volume, was newly released, so I was able to fully commit time to work with what would become a verse play, *Blood Run.* I'd studied mounds since I was a child—studied our travels, migrations, and greater blood connections. My father always persisted in attending to our awareness of the puckered continent and its historical presences under constellations gleaming and leading us on the travels and migrations we'd made over eons of existence in this very world, America, the unbroken continent prior to the building of the Panama Canal. My parents' recent DNA result patterns testify to the many peoples we bear relations to, from Patagonia, southern island nations, and the Andes up. When we were children, any time anyone would say we crossed a northern sea to arrive, he'd say, "Not us, other people did, we came from the other way, from the south," and his blood bears this story out. My father called us descendants of ballcourt people who built earthworks to mark and center their worlds as they dwelled and moved.

In the making of *Blood Run,* a sudden fury came upon me in the aftermath of a car accident in New York. I'd suffered back, neck, and brain injury that impeded me in many realms, but in this work it heightened, in some strange way, my obsession. Once I could read and write again, I worked relentlessly to strategically coordinate and compose, a methodical approach that testified to mapping the architecture of the moundscapes, constellations, propensity, and navigations of travel, and mapped traveling people returning to a cosmos center. I attempted to reveal deeper implications of the significance of the structures and their placement in the universe and of the multitudes of gatherings there. These were not personal poems, though endowed with familial or personal knowledge and research; they were attempts to speak through the vessel despite the self, to image the land, the animal and plant life able to vicariously bear witness, for the essence

of particular ghostings and remaining skeletons to be freed through lin-
gual and geometric presence in some way. It was a labor of love, and I was
enthralled and overcome—obsessed—by it. It was musical. In a sense the
work was, for me, an opus.

I received an invitation to read in Amman, Jordan, and another to read
in Medellín, Colombia, later that same year. A poet friend, Sherwin Bitsui
(Diné), had been invited and put my name forth, upon requests for nomi-
nations, to the latter event. The Medellín festival offered to bring me at the
same time as he was scheduled, so we could travel together. It was wonder-
ful to look forward to. James Thomas Stevens had already invited me to
speak at the United Nations with him in April the next year. It would be a
beautiful time in testifying to the peace theory and value of publication for
Indigenous communities, and I hoped to bring some poets from the South
to speak the year after. I went to Medellín with pleasure and hope in the
name of peace and friendship—for the poetry and the people as well as for
our shared memory.

Sherwin and I participated in the opening event with thousands in atten-
dance. Later than evening, Hugo Jamioy Juagibioy, Kamentsa (Putumayo,
Colombia), and Ariruma Kowii, Quechua (Quito, Ecuador), met us and
related their stories to us—stories of cosmology, of purpose, of war upon
them there. Hugo told me that he believed I would be "the one to connect
(them) to Indigenous poets/poetry in the North," saying that they'd studied
Sherwin's and my pictures and biographies and awaited arrival, and that
it was made obvious to them this would happen, and that they were very
happy about it. They said opportunities would come to me to do this and I
would follow through. I was thrilled to find that Ariruma's common word
for corn (or, as he said, maize) is *semu*, when *selu* is the spoken word for
corn in North Carolina. This verified for me the survival of old kinships and
trade, and I went to sleep smiling in the lingual delight.

By morning, I'd received an unexpected e-mail from Oregon State Uni-
versity inviting me to guest edit their international poetry journal *To Topos*.
They offered me an opportunity to collect an edition of poetry from "Native
America" (meaning the United States) as the geographically themed volume
I would be responsible for. As a young writer, I'd coedited two anthologies
of Indigenous college student work, and then solely edited another three
youth program editions. I was committed to presenting poetry from unsung
voices, so without much thought I replied that I would be thrilled to accept
the offer if I could make it a collection from the larger Native America,

the Indigenous America, meaning the Western Hemisphere. They agreed immediately and I began imagining and planning what this could mean.

The festival was utterly demonstrative of the absolute love of poetry as relished in most places on earth and particularly in this city, stressed by ongoing war and violence. Here, the poetry festival was the second-largest event draw, surpassed only by the annual flower festival. I fell in love with Colombia. One of the small towns, Caldez, soon became my favorite place to perform. It was beautiful. The locals referred to it as Cielo Roto (Broken Sky), since it was known to rain quite often. Hours after I read there, with a small panel of poets from all over South America, the town was overthrown by the war, and the audience displaced.

The immensity of war's effect was upon us, danger presumed nearby at any point in the city in 2005. In a neighborhood where slayings had recently occurred in its plaza, we read upon the site of the murders, the poetry cleansing the place with peace. I work in facilities of incarceration in the States, so was selected to read in the maximum-security prison in this city. So many of the faces looked familiar. I asked who in the audience was a poet as well, and about five hands went up. One young man was inside for protesting, and I invited him to read with us and to open the panel with his own work, which he did. In another venue, shots were fired throughout the reading, but no one left. It was simply target shooting, but at the reading we did not know this. Sherwin continued reading anyway, the voice for peace.

So many places within the festival locations were immensely moving. The city's botanical gardens had wonderful enormous trees said to provide invisibility to any Indigenous person in hiding, so the readings we presented there had special significance, in the urban forest. Squirrels darted up and down our shirts for handouts as if we were part of the plant world. Here was another place in which song simply overcame me. I was lifted through it.

We closed, after ten days, with a nine-hour reading, with thousands in attendance, in the same stadium we opened in. By then, there were many Indigenous poets performing from various locations included in the eighty-six poets from around the world. I cried for hours upon leaving. I cannot remember crying for any place other than homelands until that time. And I wondered if I would see our new friends alive again with their lives occupied by war. Just after the festival, I was invited to read in the World Festival of Venezuela for the next year, and I promised myself I would simply accept any South or Central American invitation I could. I hoped to create an opening to possibility between representative poets and poetry. I sent submission invitations to all the South and Central Indigenous American poets I met and asked them to spread them about to their poet-colleagues. Upon return from Medellín, I continued my work with Blood Run (both the site and the book). Northern Michigan University had offered me some funding for my research, allowing me to visit and research additional moundsites. In South Dakota, I drove west to return to annual work with the incarcerated kids in Custer and involved the students there in the wonderful story-awakenings in lingual relationships and in cultural nuances with South Americans. So many of the kids in detention are Native, the ones that are not are more easily moved when in shared quarters with Indigenous companions than in the school systems, where they are often pinned against one another in the crunched society. They were, as always, greatly interested in oratory carrying remarkable truths in the everyday, including long-removed relationships and proofs—in truths.

That spring, James and I presented at the UN, and the next summer, I traveled to read in the Venezuelan World Festival. I was able to travel to the Delta Orinoco and read with Warao poets (noticing the very apparent similarities with Seminole), and to perform in Maturín, where I met other Indigenous poets, and in Caracas (Amaranth), where the audience was cosmopolitan and multiethnic, and where I read for the first time with Mapuche poet Leonel Lienlaf and Mayan poet Jorge Cocom Pech.

Blood Run was released in the United Kingdom in late fall 2006, and in the States in 2007. *To Topos: Ahani Indigenous American Poetry,* released in early 2007, was multilingual and thick, 348 pages, yet printed so that it was easily hand-held. Arranged by stylistic and linguistic flavor, it presented poetics and linguistics of human beings as poets, for the sake of the poetry itself, in one long shared continent. The journal stood alone in the field. Both first and second print editions sold out, and a third was in the making when it became apparent that a more complete anthology was needed. Sherwin and I decided to return to read in Medellín a second time, to work with the poets there toward a statement of our joint work and continue the process of gathering ourselves as poets. In 2007, the climate had lightened amazingly, as the war was positioned farther out, so we were able to walk about as we wished, unaccompanied, and truly enjoy a much more relaxed city than Sherwin and I had visited only two years before. While in Medellín, we met other Indigenous festival poets. Hugo Jamioy Juagibioy returned specifically to read with us, and Fredy Chicangana, Gregario Gómez, Joy Harjo, Natalia Toledo, Lindantonella Solano, and Jessie Kleeman also performed in the festival, making a wonderful presentation of solidarity of Indigenous poets.

Subsequently, I arranged for one of them, Natalia Toledo (Zapoteca), to be invited to present at the UN the following year, with Linda Hogan, the newly inaugural Writer-in-Residence for the Chickasaw Nation.

I was already moving again, as I'd accepted an endowed chair in poetry and creative writing in the University of Nebraska system, and an invitation to read in the international festival at Rosario, Argentina, at about the same time, leading to more contacts with various poets from all points of the globe. It was frustrating to realize how much great poetry we were missing in existing representative volumes, how much we were separated from one another in the canon. I wanted to make a space for that connection and made the proposal to the University of Arizona, submitting the journal as the abstract, and then began collecting what would become this volume from especially significant works that previously existed in *To Topos* while eliciting a new call to expand and develop the presentation. Around this time the University of California at Santa Cruz contacted me and requested my poet contacts from Central and South America, to invite them to perform in a festival/conference they wanted to host on campus. Many of the poets I'd worked with in the South happily traveled to read there with Indigenous poets from North America. Meanwhile, I continued gathering poets on the U.S. pampas (Quechua word for *grasslands/plains*) for the Sandhill Crane convergence and World Affairs Conferences.

My new work, in Nebraska, included directing the Reynolds Reading Series of Visiting Writers, wherein we began to immediately widen the university's James E. Smith World Affairs Conference by bringing some of these same South American poets as the conference's first representative Indigenous American voices, as well as a poet laureate of Cuba, Nancy Morejón, and a Nigerian poet, Chris Abani. The conference occurs just prior to a writer's retreat and festival I founded, upon arrival, to honor the epicenter of the Sandhill Crane migration, here, on the Platte River Valley, where we now bring in many Indigenous and other poets and writers who share affinity and cultural and lingual signifiers from these very birds in the crux of the annual migration. Some of these poets' subsequent work is included herein, and some published in the *Platte Valley Review*. Lise Erdrich joined us as an Anishinaabe writer who has studied some of the traditional crane scribing from the ancient and continuous written Indigenous language resulting from impressions of these ancient and contemporary birds. Her work, like the work of the oratory collectors to the south, is imperative to the conversation of a much wider base for all contemporary Indigenous poets composing in the Americas. New, yes, in a contemporary sense, but with far-ranging particles of legacy.

In working to configure the collection of this anthology, it was important to consider several phenomenal multigenre/poetic existing contemporary works collected by anthologists Kim Blaeser, Joe Bruchac, Heid E. Erdrich, Diane Glancy, Joy Harjo, Maurice Kenny, Duane Niatum, Simon Ortiz, Laura Tohe, Anna Lee Walters, and others, and, as gifted by my parents, an early childhood copy of *The Winged Serpent,* all of which influenced the making of this representative assemblage. This volume, more specifically, stems from my travels in the larger field, and from the original editorial engagement with *To Topos: Poetry International,* as editors Eric Wayne Dickey and Joseph Ohmann-Krause provided the timely invitation for me to guest edit an edition representing American Indian and First Nations poetry that was negotiated into the more inclusive volume of Indigenous poetry from the Arctic Inupiat to Mapuche in Chile. *Ahani* was, perhaps, the first journal edition of its kind. Several of the most moving and poetically effective pieces from that collection are included here as conceptual base, as continuing testimony to the inaugural work and experience from just a few years ago. Here, in *Sing,* the conversation continues and expands into a formal anthology, including a broadened, amazingly diverse host of poets set to enkindle readers to investigate these poetics, poems, and to make these poets' work familiar in scholarly research and educational study, engendered literary discourse, and recreational personal pleasure.

It is my hope that this compilation serves as an inlet to immense diversity in orality, linguistic, and cultural sway of individual contemporary poets as individually talented poets, whose significantly illustrative and representative poetry is gathered here collectively but maintains the dignity and integrity of each poet as individual throughout. This attempt does tender a smidgen of the communalities, commonalities, and distinct diverseness demonstrated in lingual constructions, endowed with rich poetic revelation in the celebration and fragility of human condition, in its spirited, elegiac, challenging, or profound manifestation experienced as life in the Occidental Hemisphere. This includes not only intertribal, but also some examples of intercultural, poet conversation, with three poems paying tribute to Whitman, for instance, who was said to be inspired by Indigenous poetry/oratory of his own time and time before him.

This book is meant to be neither a manifesto nor a completely comprehensive volume, but an assertion of significant presence of continual literary and lyric engagement, as an edifying representative field survey of some of the finest poets publishing today in the Indigenous Americas. It is a selected volume. Many contributors are proven poets, nationally or internationally acclaimed, published, and actively involved. Other contributors are freshly appearing in the literary scene. Their respective contributions to this collection are essential in providing a volume specifically generated to sample from the incredible diversity and breadth of poets with tribal citizenry, heritage, and/or descent pertaining to the Indigenous Western Hemisphere. Additional measure has been mediated, at times, to poets who live in situational and imminent danger, merited in respect to their duress and necessary work, with special attention to poets whose communities experience siege from right/left national, international, and paramilitaries, as in Colombia and Chile. Their work needs be known, and I have dedicated more page count because of this concern.

As with anything along pathways of reconnection and reunification, step-by-step progress is made through word of mouth and offering of hands or hugs in friendship or shared purpose. In the multitudes of eons of flourishing liaisons and relationships in America, as a whole continent, the peoples populating the Western Hemisphere enjoyed their travels and revelations, migrations and lingual sharings, as well as social and ceremonial times together. In this work, something similar has happened. This volume is a unification of sorts, a steady drive to reconnect and proliferate the field with the current poetics by descendants of the original inhabitants of America in all her longevity and full length as a continent, thus unbroken in spirit and fortitude in the poetics presented here.

As no funds were available to support the work, and with so much personal out-of-pocket expense, I was unable to compensate additional poets whose work I would have enjoyed including. Some of these poets represented countries that are not present herein, as a result. Though this is an inclusive volume, meant to provide a survey of the field, it is in no way an absolute volume, nor does it contain work from each nation in the Americas, no more than an eastern-hemispheric anthologized collection would encompass all nations representing the Eastern Hemisphere. Much of this is due to cost, but a great portion of the issue is colonial separation and lack of fluid contemporary cultural exchange in the Americas due to existing underlying politics. *Poetry Like Bread* (Martin Espada, Curbstone Press, 1994) was an exceptional collection, remembered fondly, with significant representation of poetry (thirty-three poets) from the Americas and other continents, though focused mainly on non-Indigenous poets. I am unaware of a current comprehensive volume representing poets from all of the Americas, Indigenous or not. In a perfect world, these things could easily be remedied, and we would have volumes and volumes of highly comprehensive value available readily in curriculum from grade school up. As it is, this may be the largest collective representation of literature from the Indigenous Americas that is completely composed of contemporary poetry. I hope to be a part of this continued realization, or at least to witness the making of such incredible future books; now, at least, the conversation is initiated and punctuated, and survey volumes, including this one, are available. Some selections I accepted (and adored) from contributing poets were also cut for page count, to meet the publisher's requested criteria in this volume; and for this I send hope for future editions.

Additionally, I had to rely heavily upon Eric Dickey (OSU) in the initial stages of securing permissions for poems accepted in *Ahani* and added soon thereafter. I also relied heavily upon my son Travis Hedge Coke to assist with additional calls for submissions, selection, collation, securing translators, and typesetting the manuscript. Luckily for me, he graduated MFA from the University of California Riverside–Palm Desert and began teaching down the hall here just in time to become a major assistant in this work. I feel fortunate to have someone so close, so willing to get his hands into the mess of manuscript making. Additionally, the phenomenal translators all volunteered their tremendous efforts to create this volume. For the multilingual sections, nearly half of the volume, containing most of the Indigenous poets south of the States, the poets most often wrote in both Indigenous language and Spanish. As this book attempts to provide some aspect of field impression, the works must be presented in the specified dominant language for the poets' respective countries, and in Indigenous language, to honor their own experience with language, before translating to English for the lay reader in the United States and Canada. Thus, most of the inclusions herein were translated into English from Spanish and the respective Indigenous language. Most of the translators are well-known poets (poetry great Juan Felipe Herrera among them) and notable writers in their own right (wolf reclamationist, Mexican writer-biologist Cristina Eisenberg), and some are emerging as writers and already working as professional translators. Some of the translators are from the same countries as the poet they translated. All are Spanish-language speakers, most in the first-language or dual-language sense. Their work is essential to this edition. Language order was as suggested by each contributing poet. Some poems in this section are in one language and are included strictly due to the stylistic compatibility therein.

The other half of the volume is filled with contributing poets from northern North America, primarily the United States. Access to a larger grouping here was possible due to editorial location, access, and gross knowledge of the field at hand. This bulk in no way implies favoritism, but rather more ease of availability and common knowledge, and attempts to show an expansion of the (available) early-twenty-first-century breadth in this section of the Americas. Balance will likely improve over the next few decades of editing, as we are coming closer and closer through technologies and opportunities such as world festivals inviting participation from Indigenous communities of poets, so our connections grow and reestablish, and the poetry becomes more available.

The volume is collected in seven representative sections of corresponding poetic conversation customarily collected in stylistic approach, tone, intent, relative content, challenge, device, and literary value.

"Prelude" introduces the reading as "Calyx" forms the whorl enclosing the petals (flower of knowledge) that serve to protect the budding poetic awakening the volume strives toward. It is the invocation of the text, the overture, as "Calyx" delivers essential preparatory instructions to the reader and, in a traditional sense, establishes approach.

> Kneeling before the altar of your hands
> you close your eyes and listen to wooden sunbeams
> splinter dirt floors into peninsulas of ice,
> each crackle—
> a fissure blooming dove wings fluttering past the stone
>   on which you sharpened your teeth,
> as if cornering the wolves
>   snarling when you ask to leave your hair bandaged
> would shut windows opened to green pastures
> and plume your palm with brown skin.

The naturally camouflaged "Ptarmigan" represents the intention to espouse poetic cloaking through imagery, metaphor, murmur, and singing quality of verse (intentional and/or innate), lyrically and philosophically opening the negotiation of reader entrance into the text, while providing the base connection for the sustaining volume. These lines from Cathy Tagnak

Rexford, in "The Ecology of Subsistence," exemplify this repetitive measure of the volume:

> Her hairline marks her shift   from caribou to woman.
> Standing in front of three white spotlights
> the silhouette of five black arrowheads
> departs from her lips.
>
>> Splice together her eyelashes and
>> frozen lids   exaggerate the strain
>> of her freckles coiled into song.
>
> Inukshuks tumble from the tips of her fingernails
> guiding the landing strip for twin otters;
> they watch their children travel to the moon,
>> or perhaps they erase our oiled webs.

"Liminal" offers temporal threshold poetry, poetry of impression, strategic challenge, transitional call, and dualistic presentation. This movement provides the reader with initiation in the nuance of awakening and defiance. It demonstrates portal view into contemporary parallel existences and departures.

In Laura Tohe's "blue book #5," a strange continuity derives from separate sides of a shared moon, now divided. In this acuity, each viewer must persist, and carry on, beyond the split transition:

> half of your moon hangs on your side of the world
>
>> mine hangs outside my bedroom window
>
> where the cicadas sing the last of their summer songs
>
>> in the desert night
>
> soon they will sing us into   another season then leave us
>
> and I will be left to make my way and you yours

"Ñeñe'i Ha-ṣa:gid (In the Midst of Songs)" opens aetheric, unbound, linguistic expanse, embracing multilingual works, borderless, in whistling mosaic. The arc is movement, motion below and above ground—flying.

"Earth Movement," by Ofelia Zepeda, details the levitation necessary to lifting and the song-induced method of release.

> Her visualization so strong
> She can almost feel her body arch against the centrifugal force of the
>   rotation
> She can see herself with her long hair floating
> Floating in the atmosphere of stardust
> She rides her planet the way a child rides a toy
> Her company is the boy who takes the sun on its daily journey
> And the man in the moon smiles as she passes by.

"Sobre los Campos (Through the Fields)" specifically regards experiential poetry of sovereign authenticity in sweeping original and traditional migratory landscapes, including multilingual poetry of conflict, lament, celebration, and task chantey. A crescendo builds throughout this measure, allowing the reader a closer personal relationship with necessary work by poets dealing with life-and-death issues in everyday beingness and in actual violent conflict due to current wars on traditional homelands, a *now* that exemplifies history in the making, as sobering as the opening poem, "Bajan Gritando Ellos Sobre los Campos," by Leonel Lienlaf:

> Wirarünmu nagpay yengün
> Iweñünmu küpaley yen gün
> Pepan ñi pu che
> Umül-umülü-yengün
> Wente Mapu
> Wentemew rupay pu winka
> Allfüli ti mapu yengün
> Allfüli ñi piuke
>
> Bajan gritando
> ellos sobre los campos
> silbando por los esteros
> corro a ver a mi gente,
> a mi sangre
> pero ya están tendidos
> sobre el suelo

sobre ellos pasan los winkas/huincas
hiriendo de muerte la tierra,
dividiendo mi corazón

They come down yelling
through the fields
whistling through the marshes
I run to see my people
my blood
but they are already lying
on the floor
over them the white men walk
fatally wounding the land
splitting up my heart

"The List We Make" generously endows the reading with ease into representational colloquial and vernacular song and sites rendered in these contemporary poetics. List poems, instructional and explanatory pieces, recipes, wishes, laments, tributes, elegy, comedy, numbered, reels, calendar pages, and counting for the sake of incantation, chant, or catalogue—an ordinate approach to poetry. Included as assertion, an accounting of experience and gathered knowns, experiential knowledge gained, what must now be shed and held onto. This is deliverance from attachment and incantatory recall for future worth. Infused throughout is a sense of levity, as in "Simple Four Part Directions for Making Indian Lit," by Gordon Henry:

Make crossing tongues
As simple as pow wow for profit
And dying chevy hey yaw
As complex as Aristotle remains ethical
And remains remain catalogued
Use newspapers, magazines, museum brochures,
Skatagon, flint and match
Roll characters, names words, onto paper
Paper into rolls
Rub with beargrease and lard,
Or last night's ground beef leavings

(this will not work with
Olive or sunflower oil)
Say four hail marys, a couple of
Aho's or ah ah kaweekin
Ignite all of the above

"Sing You Back," the paean anthem of reclamation, harbors poetry with homing device and lullaby closure. This section provides the finale, declarative resolve, resolution, leading into concord, the course of harmonic change— infinitive. The regular editors of *To Topos: Poetry International* told me to include a piece of my own to close the guest-edited edition *Ahani*. I included the poem I'd originally composed for Medellín, because the editorial work immediately resulted therefrom. For most of the University of Arizona Press reviewers of the journal, submitted as evidence to propose this new anthology, "America, I Sing You Back" was noted as aesthetically relevant to the workings of any new collection.

The poem was suggested to serve in the final section title herein, and as final inclusion, with the exception of one reviewer (post–anthology manuscript submission) who preferred the new volume end—as it does—with a new inclusion, a wonderful return poem by Duane Niatum. While initially uncomfortable including my own work, after looking over extant Indigenous (poetry inclusive) anthologies, I came to realize that each volume did include contributions from the editor, most toward the finality of the read. (Unlike in the mainstream lit scene, the last position is not a position of rank, but one of humility). In the interest of continuity and relative poetic conversation in the community, and by suggestion of the University of Arizona Press senior editor, I eventually included "America, I Sing You Back" in this new volume. It has become a tribute, for me, to the cyclical return of my own initiative to reach throughout the larger America in conversational verse, to my reasoning that we are all in this together and must put matters and any concern for grace of ego completely aside. My work as editor has not been apart from the contributing poets, but from a part of the mass included and gathered here. With the inclusion of crane poems from our retreat of witness of the epicenter on the Platte (by Linda Hogan and Fredy Chicangana, while other Crane Fest writers included in this volume are LeAnne Howe, James Thomas Stevens, Janet McAdams, Hugo Jamioy Juagibioy, Laura Tohe, Sherwin Bitsui, Travis Hedge Coke, Lise Erdrich, and translator Cristina Eisenberg), I've also added "Platte Mares" to testify to the great gathering cycle of migratory birds and the duality of nomenclature, where I begin to make associative leaps and, in this instance, where female mustangs and cranes are both referred to as mares and their offspring colts. This focus, through the migration, testifies to our now annual international poet gatherings here on the migratory staging grounds of the Platte River as a measure of bringing us collectively to one of the many centers in America, bringing us all back to something greater than ourselves as individuals— bringing us home.

In "Riding the Wake of the Paddle Journey," Duane Niatum gives the reader an exemplary sense of return to belongingness in a deeper sense of home—

> Laxaynam, our canoe, parts the water
> the way waves pass through wind currents,
>   curl back upon themselves.
>
> This island passage is a body of voices
> and salmon swimming beside us. We will
>   hear the animal people and eagles
>
> each winter ceremony and in the fathoms
> of sleep. We glide over whitecaps as Sea Wolf
>   chants and channels our blood
>
> in the paddles' thrust. In the wake of our guardian
> we return to this path to be servants of our ghosts,
>   the family keeping the storytelling stone
>
> that shows our flesh's formed by tide and stump.

—and closes the book with a collective directive, and presents the pathway of return in a spiritual sense as well:

> Drifting to the beach, we point our paddles toward
> the white trail in the sky, honor Xaʔeʔf, the Changer,
>   and the mountain keeping our heart
>
> as broad and deep as the red elderberry sky.
> We honor the hosts, the Puyallups, our family,
>   children, and elders greeting us from shore;

their drum and song a sunlight flame circles
the birth of water stories, the smokehouse path
        of sun, wolf, and Thunderbird.

It is here the volume reaches an overtone, some complex oscillation denoting vibration, resonance. Here, we remake ourselves in the simplicity of return, be it metaphorical or literal, depending on the read. Or, in the traditional phrasing, "make ourselves over," by uniting with and paying tribute to the place(s) from which we come. That arrival is always with song, and the song itself makes it so. Typically, in the traditional sense, either a new name might be given or validation of an existing name would have been made in the journey, thus a new beginning born from finality, or proof.

I had not considered working with a new title when embarking upon this collection. I was thoroughly attached to the ideology of *Ahani* ("here," placement referring to the actual shared—versus separated—continent, pre–Panama Canal) and ultimately wished to expand this notion. Once the sections of the new collection were arranged for readability, by stylistic and aesthetic poetic approach—thus creating the expansive thread I originally sought to deliver—the resulting overall narrative produced a remarkably obvious title. *Sing* represents the repetitive, edifying inclusion of musicality and the many aspects of use of song in Indigenous cultures throughout the hemisphere, and song is thus present by nature throughout the collection. The multiple-millennia use of song as portico, as navigational instrument, as labor initiative, nourishment, and mechanism for endurance, and as ceremonial healing expedient for tens of thousands of generations of millions and millions of people, provides contemporary cultural conditioning and continual benefit for the future as well. This conception (post-collection) provided a welcome epiphany for me, especially in that it presented itself despite me and made sense in the way that does distinguish a notion of comprehensive ideology. So many necessary things in life present themselves in this way. We often need step out of the way for the best ideas to formulate. The thoughts, the means, are there for us to collide into once the ego is put in its proper place. Here, the generative title works to interleave the volume which is basic, prime, known and serves to recognize the instance that illustrates a gross connectivity for many of the cultures represented herein. A ceremony meant to direct a process is known as a Sing, in that the methodology of the ceremony is entirely strategized and orchestrated through a series of songs, and the art and act of singing those particular movements create the place for possibility overall. In my work as a poet, it has been a great honor and privilege to work with this volume. Having dedicated myself to tribute of the traditional earthworks of ballcourt peoples, original throughout the Americas, and in my larger attempt to reunite contemporary Indigenous poets with the impression and influence of the sandhill crane and other migratory birds in the Americas, with one another's poetry, constructions, cultural migrations, and traditional homes, this work is tribute to the continual literary work of millions of Indigenous people in the lands of millions and millions of migratory and settled birds, puckered with millions of mounds laid in tribute, testimony, and homage, for all to know. Here is a bit of the music.

Prelude

Sherwin Bitsui

Calyx

Kneeling before the altar of your hands
you close your eyes and listen to wooden sunbeams
splinter dirt floors into peninsulas of ice,
each crackle—
a fissure blooming dove wings fluttering past the stone
        on which you sharpened your teeth,
as if cornering the wolves
        snarling when you ask to leave your hair bandaged
would shut windows opened to green pastures
and plume your palm with brown skin.

*

Amber barn light flashes upon orange rinds worming through the cow's skull,

ivory columns of smoke followed by silk curtains billow from our eyelids,

scattering snow over the cliff's edge, we know for some reason, reason was here.

The night, our cornfield's glittering backdrop, splatters the windshield and we
        are flung

back towards dust, our minds forked with spilled ink tasting like turtle blood
        under our

hushed bodies.

*

How do I describe her daubing my face with cornhusk?

Ptarmigan

Cathy Tagnak Rexford

The Ecology of Subsistence

No daylight for two months, an ice chisel slivers
frozen lake water refracting blue cinders.

By light of an oil lamp, a child learns to savor marrow:
cracked caribou bones a heap on the floor.

A sinew, thickly wrapped in soot, threads through
the meat on her chin: a tattoo in three slender lines.

One white ptarmigan plume fastened to the lip of
a birch wood basket; thaw approaches: the plume turns brown.

On the edge of the open lead, a toggle-head harpoon
waits to launch: bowhead sings to krill.

Thickened pack ice cracking; a baleen fishing line
pulls taut a silver dorsal fin of a round white fish.

A slate-blade knife slices along the grain of a caribou
hindquarter; the ice cellar lined in willow branches is empty.

Saltwater suffuses into a flint quarry, offshore
a thin layer of radiation glazes leathered walrus skin.

Alongside shatters of a hummock, a marsh marigold
flattens under three black toes of a sandhill crane.

A translucent sheep horn dipper skims a freshwater stream;
underneath, arctic char lay eggs of mercury.

Picked before the fall migration, cloudberries
drench in whale oil, ferment in a sealskin poke.

A tundra swan nests inside a rusted steel drum;
she abandons her newborns hatched a deep crimson.

Baleen Scrimshaw as 16 mm Film

Shoot in 16 mm film, capture her sitting under
an olive-green archway.
       Loop the sound of steel striking glass.
When you blink, the camera captures
the frame of her kin, walking upside down.
       Loop the sound of tundra grass sprouting.

Her hairline marks her shift   from caribou to woman.
Standing in front of three white spotlights
the silhouette of five black arrowheads
departs from her lips.

       Splice together her eyelashes and
       frozen lids   exaggerate the strain
       of her freckles coiled into song.

Inukshuks tumble from the tips of her fingernails
guiding the landing strip for twin otters;
they watch their children travel to the moon,
       or perhaps they erase our oiled webs.

       Chart sixteen luminaries into the Beaufort Sea.
       Wait.   Wait.   Wait.
         The shutter will remember
           their white crested etchings.

They resurface in the lyric of your documentary.

James Thomas Stevens

Isère

As unaccustomed as I am
to lights at such height,
I marvel at perceived
                    aeroplanes
coming toward your kitchen window
                            at night.

Lights of a town
on mountaintop, really.

Someone
in his warm home in Saint Nizier
must be peering
                down
                        to this glowing bowl.

Unaware of my dark silhouette
as it draws inward
when you enter, your hand at the base of my back.

Unaware, that some months later
an obscuring cloud
will descend the Vercors
                        and she will have no name.

But today, nescient and traversing
the Chemin du Bois d'artas,
I remark on the gates of
                    a playground,
the frothy swell of spheres
in bas relief
            on cold stone posts.

You laugh. You say, *I have never noticed,*
and the heavy walls of the park, pregnant
with the years of your children's laughter,
                    accept your laughter too.

While rows of old stone houses threaten to lift and drift away.

It happens when you're waiting
or walking over a bridge,
while standing at the base
       of a mountain green as Chartreuse.

All pulleys and cables pulling
the curious to the crest
in our creaturely constant desire for height

      . . . best view, best sight, best, farthest, beyond the
   Belledonne.

I see an image
        of us inverted,
above
      the winding *Isère,*
            reflected in our small
                  glass
                    gondola.

   Chimerical *us,* floating above the city.

Brandy Nālani McDougall

Hāloa Naka

There is no need to sweeten
        your body's ripe offering
to suit my open mouth.

        I take you in, as you are—
    the taste of earth and light,
        salt-wind sieved through valley rains.

        Just days ago, your heart-
           shaped leaves faced the sun,
        funneling light and warmth

        through your long trembling
           stalks. You felt the soft earth
        open itself to your roots,

      whose blind strands fed
        the crystalline nebulae
      that once purpled your corm.

Still, you give yourself over
and over again, e hiapo,

your sacrifice made ripe
in the soil's short incubation—

so that we may live knowing love
and 'ohana, our bright belonging.

The History of This Place

Here, there are no visible remnants
    impressing the grass,
            no rock piles
to mark the many passings

to which this place bore witness,
    housing the salt
            of tears, of bone
under the canopy of palai ferns.

There is only the spirit of memory
    that stirs the air,
            dark and heavy
like a broth strained from the living

body of *before,* saturating the earth,
    the rain sinking
            the old grief

down deep, closer to the fire within.

Louise Erdrich

White Braids

Her family slept beneath the quilts she made
of mission coats and Bull Durham tobacco bags,
each square washed, pressed, sewn.
She made offerings to the thunders. They were good to her.
They did not take any of her children before she died.

I saw her afterwards, dancing her special category.
One hundred years and over jingle dress exhibition in the stars.
Her dress was made with cones of 925 silver.
They rippled against the black cloth.
Her tough little feet stabbed the clouds,
each step like a needle pricking up beads.

You have to stay skinny to dance that long.
You have to go easy on the bannock and jelly and wine.
You have to make to die in such a way
that you take no one with you. Leave everyone behind.
At peace. Tie up all the loose ends
the way a good beadworker threads the last stitch
back into the pattern.

Crow

Where are you taking me, mysterious one?
Down what path? What road of life?

Thunder in the morning
I am motionless, traveling

and it is bitter—this love that gives me no rest
but sends me into the heart of things

though I am not certain who waits there,
you, or the longing.

And if this love is not a human love
and if I cannot hold your hand in the night
then what is it?

Thunder out of the south.
Clouds boiling over the rim of the earth.

You, black feathers,
or my body, this circle of forgetfulness,
taking flight?

dg nanouk okpik

Sinnaktuq (Dream)

Along the breakwater
she walks alone,
then kneels, throat singing
cupping her hands to the brook.
She sleeps—
walking in blackish light
awakes when *apun* is lowest.

Her knuckles are whitish red,
in the silt ice water dragging,
across sharp flint,
yet like bone toggles where flesh
meets sinew across the Beaufort Sea.

(maybe it was her home at Birnirk that kept her there.)

Her house at the edge of the spit,
stands on peeling driftwood stilts.
the Coleville river lapses and folds,
then culls the shoreline.

In her eyes the constant fuse
of the narrow, long, path jumps
into slate hands in gelid tones of re-tracing,
she dreams electric eels, oil lamps, bone tools,
used for mooring a *umiak* with a twine of grass.

Her hands track and pluck the baseline,
of skin which holds tendons, piece meal
of ribbed aluminum and sod roofs.
Each night an inua opens flashed windows
of the old Quonset hut to let the air out.

She's using a harpoon to trammel,
etching the fissure of ground,
each line a place to name, a clan sword
to shorten the permafrost by adding a piece.

So many thermals of wind,
to hit the hemmed dam upstream,
like a gaff clutched by blink movements.

(If she decreases the height of the pictograph,
will it make caribou roam on scrimshaw?)

She waits for the midnight sun,
to bleach a seal skin—slowly it comes.
Comes in blotches of wild cotton grass,
on solar planks on roofs to collect sod flowers.
An oil drum elongates and cleans the drifts
like buoys floating on the ocean carried
by great auks and purple martin.
It is said in that moment the script began.

On Poetics

> But finding no resting place, returned; then I sent forth a raven.
> The raven flew off, and seeing that the waters had decreased,
> [Cautiously] waded in the mud, but did not return. . . .
> —*The Epic of Gilgamesh*

I

When the mud dried black spruce culled
at the river's lapse, I slouched over to fill my mouth—
the ice pack gorge flowed over my fingers.
I cupped then drank. Right hand first, left followed.
Is this the way to the earth? I've stood still
but the sea and sky kept circling, circling
the midnight sun, I did not return.

II

In the loft, I found one carved wing of yellow cedar
resting at the bottom of the netted cage.
Foul and cold air swept by me. Aaka called,
I dropped the wooden wing, fled down the ladder
to a black bird in a mask. A box of suet spilled.
I ran to the river to meet the ocean's edge.
I returned at dusk.

III

Ellipse of the moon when the sun is the lowest—
harp, timpani, bass viol, flute,
wavelengths of woodwinds.
The nimbus darkened, a gingko fan leaf
measured candela carbon in the expanse,
Genesis at dense blithe. The bell on the mountain
rang beyond the scape: echo, echo.

IV

Blackfish parr, swimmer of freshwater—
urn of eggs pocketed in rocks.
Swimmer flow past in this moon
for you—brackish seasons leap.
So it is, you breathe quantum lux
and return, return, and return.

Elise Paschen

Magnificent Frigatebird

Slapdash of waves. White onyx moon. Sea turtles
crack out of shells beneath the sand while overhead

ocean birds, like ampersands, punctuate
the sky. *Conjoin, conjoin.* They link earthbound

Sentences—*How long to walk on this ground?
How short our stay?*—during that man-o'-war

struggle between the dirt and air. *Which part
to keep? Which part to give away?* I celebrate

your birth, stretching out half a century,
while you read outside the sea grass hut, minutes

before the end of day. Perched on the deck,
interrogating the sun, I look up.

Above, a Magnificent Frigatebird
hovers mid-air, his silhouetted shape,

a tilde symbol. Beneath his superscription
we're grounded, transfixed, as if his swung dash

marked this spot on the sand or else transformed
the articulation of every limb.

As if we were some notes on a keyboard
waiting to be altered into a sound

or chord never practiced. I try to read
the horizon. Your voice roots out my name.

Barn Owl and Moon

Night-fall, we stretch and tumble under rafters,
beneath the moon. Bats' breath against our lips.
     The barn owl and the moon.

A scream, a snore, a hiss, a click, a scratch.
Duets of eyes ignite, burn out the night.

Your heart-shaped face, talons, and tawny skin.
My crescent arc—waxing—all marrow, pearl.

Fixed in the sky. A scythe. Afraid to cut.
We hide. This flash might blind and talons strip.

It's dark. A drumbeat of feathers scales up
my spine. Rapt, out-of-breath, we tilt, take wing.

You clasp a shell of skin. I shed more light
tucked between claw and claw. Rise above earth:
     the barn owl and the moon.

Wí'-gi-e

    Anna Kyle Brown. Osage.
    1896–1921. Fairfax, Oklahoma.

Because she died where the ravine falls into water.

Because they dragged her down to the creek.

In death, she wore her blue broadcloth skirt.

Though frost blanketed the grass she cooled her feet in the spring.

Because I turned the log with my foot.

Her slippers floated downstream into the dam.

Because, after the thaw, the hunters discovered her body.

Because she lived without our mother.

Because she had inherited head rights for oil beneath the land.

She was carrying his offspring.

The sheriff disguised her death as whiskey poisoning.

Because, when he carved her body up, he saw the bullet hole in her skull.

Because, when she was murdered, the *leg clutchers* bloomed.

But then froze under the weight of frost.

During *Xtha-cka Zhi-ga Tse-the*, the *Killer of the Flowers Moon*.

I will wade across the river of the blackfish, the otter, the beaver.

I will climb the bank where the willow never dies.

M. L. Smoker

Equilibrium

In memory of Eric Levi Big Leggins

1.

After child after child after child, no one
believes in the cacophony of sirens any more.

If only we could break back these bones
and form a new ceremony from all of our losses.

O' mend our teeth from another dark stretch of road,
our rugged knuckles from another first of the month.

2.

And still, the children keep jumping from trains.
The people in town dream anxiously,
fire and iron licking at the corners of old,
handmade quilts. They have forgotten
the language of antelope and creek bed,
find in its place only one way to say
we are not responsible.

Today one man woke to the callous offering
of a bird's beak and black wing,
left on his doorstep at daybreak.
And what of all the other warnings,
of all the family lost because their hearts
were too heavy for them to carry?
If we could put these omens away, down in the basement
the door could be locked,
the mutter of crows left there to decay.

3.

Next time and it will be the dance
of chairs and imaginary high speed chases.
It will require a fine sense of balance
and a song of stars.
Just the slightest slip of the rope
and the sky will be set
loose, the body
like a shift in the river's current.

4.

The bridge can hold, the body can not, and our excuses
will do nothing to save us now.

We survive between these barbed wire
fabrications. We gather together in the middle of the night,
call out the names of lost cousins and friends who cannot
cross over to the other side because we keep
praying them back.
We ask so much of them: *slow the car down, don't jump
don't let go, come back to us.*

But what are we really guilty of?—the blood memory of what
we can't forgive ourselves for.

5.

Hollowed out grief becomes electric,
loosens a thousand storm patterns
in the marrow of ghost homes,
ghost children, ghost love.

Back Again

There are Indian women crying in the bathroom of Arlo's bar,
busted up, I guess—"you shouldn't a messed with him again."
They're in there for so long we almost forget about them.
A trail of cigarette smoke edging its way along the crack near
the floor is the only reminder that they are still here.
Maybe it takes that closed up behind a locked door feeling
to get them through another round. Mervyn asks the white guys
at the pool table if they want to play a game for their lives.
He grins and lets out his *Braveheart* cry, so loud the whole bar
turns to see. He isn't afraid of much and maybe he knows
that playing for it all is the only way to go. The white guys don't
know any better, so they accept his challenge. He lands every shot
and one by one, they realize what a mistake they've made.
They wonder about the wager, edge their way up to the bar and
finally disappear out the front door. In the neon light of a Coors sign
Mervyn does his own victory dance around the pool table,
and maybe each step reminds him that he is the one still standing.

Maurice Kenny

Arts Poetica

I won't write of violets blooming
in the woods anymore. No sweet spring
ever-returning to the mountains.

I may want to write of great deeds
and great deed do-ers, or my ten toes
twitching in sudsy waters of a hot tub,
or how many whiskers my cat sees
darkness with, or how to make broccoli
less boring. The good thing about Bush . . .
he too thought broccoli odious.

Oh! and I don't want to be political
anymore. I shall cease cursing Custer,
and promise never to write alliteration
ever again because its sounds plotted.
Much too classical for my tastes.

But it really is the spring violets
which get my goat, get my dander up.
If violets or daffodils could
sprout in a crusty crotch then maybe
I'd start to write about violets again.

Even suicide is not worthy of a poem
though I may consider it often,
or the dream in which my father appears
and guides me through the walk of life.

What shall I write of, are
hairy armpits and dead gardens,
bad Hollywood movies and folks
who I don't like very much.

And so did Whitman, Housman, Millay and Who Knows What Other Crazy Poet Did . . .

I sing of marigolds
      and
          no
             one gives a damn.
I sing of blue mornings
      and
          they wish
             I would not
They don't want dawns nor blossoms
in their brief days and long nights
    Let's have another Bud, fellows
I sing dandelions
            who cares
I sing black-eyed-susans
            who gives a damn
I sing of purple lupine
            and masturbating
               boys
            pull them off the plant
            to stamp them out
    and the seeds fall to the winds
          to the winds of the four corners
              the seven seas
          the winds sweep the seeds away
          as night sweeps the twilight
          as mama sweeps the dust out the door
          the seeds scatter
               boys multiply

I sing of purple lupine, morning marigolds
I sing of freshness, newness, originality
and no one cares
not
even the boys
or the flushed cheek of June

I sing of hate, murder, blood and death
and
no one
and no one cares, no one . . .

Orlando White

Ars Poetica

He gave me a book and I opened it. The first line I noticed was, "The child with the blank face of an egg." Then, I felt my face erased to its skull.

There was a missing space. So I peeled off a piece of a letter from the next page. And I nudged it carefully between the i and j.

She said, "How does it feel to have your head stuck in a zero?" Silence in a moment is imagination and I replied, "It is my halo."

I erased a zero and it appeared in someone else's thoughts. The sum of a zero and zero is zero. I wrote it again; this time it made sense.

He said, "We raise it to the lips of the nearest ear." So, I began to open books, listen for ink boiling, the scent of words, coffee brewing in my ear.

I watched the clock as if reading a sentence. The numbers were letters. The short hand was a subject, the long hand, a predicate, and the seconds, a verb.

We both stared at the ceiling. I said, "My eyes feel as if they're inside cups." Then she said, "Shall I pour your eyes back into your ears?"

Language structures what we see without saying it. But I began to pull bones from sentences, and rearrange letters into skeletons.

I heard a circle as if it were a clock. It did not tick; made the sound of an insect: it was a number in the shape of a cricket.

I opened an envelope addressed to me. I pulled out a blank sheet of paper, unfolded it. In the letter: no message, no sender's name, just a white space.

"I like that you exist," she said. Like the lowercase i, my body felt present on a page: fitted in a dark suit, white necktie, and inside the black dot, a smile.

But it was the way her skin felt as she dressed into a black outfit. The way her body slipped into a long dark dress shaped like a shadow.

He picked up a stone; held it to his ear. Shook it like a broken watch. He opened it, and inside were small gears, shaped like a clock.

I am a skeleton, a sentence, too. Although like you, I am neither a meaning nor a structure, just silence in a complete thought.

Atsíísts'in

Below the skull there is part of a letter

shaped like a bone. But the skull is not a skull;

it is a black dot with white teeth. And the piece

of the letter under it is not really a bone,

rather a dark spine. This is not the end of language.

When it was alive it had a ribcage;

each rib taken out by small pincers

the way strands of eyelash are removed

from eyelids. And the dot used to have eyes—

white like two grains of salt. But they were dissolved

by two drops of ink. The way a letter fades

on the page after many years of reading

or how it soaks into a fingerprint and forgets itself.

The way a word tries to breathe inside

a closed book; the way a letter shivers when

a page is turned. Because underneath sound

there is thought. Language, a complete structure

within the white coffin of paper. If you shake it

and listen, it will move, rattle like bones on the page.

Tiffany Midge

Stories Are Alive Beings

The moon is my cup.
I drink the stars down.
Night is hot liquid steeped in clouds,
poured from the hands of planets.
Someone beautiful told me
Stories are alive beings,
little animals who drink from the creek
of my spirit; who scratch at the door;
who invent absurd and curious ways
of being in the world; who
carve indelible maps in the sky
for the rest of us to follow.

At the Fish Ladder

Beyond the river called logic
salmon climb a ladder to the stars.

It is that place where the harvester
of dreaming combs out his hair,

and where the birthing of planets
surges into indelible perceptions.

Oil Spill

Monte, Laura's man, just got back from a three-
week Louisiana bird rescue; pelicans.
Laura who has drawn and painted birds for years
was making a nest for Monte all along,
before she ever met him, her sparrow bones
felt him in the air and she migrated north
for the long summer of love. In her studio
I finger pelican bones, mollusk shells,
a piece of down; I cherry pick through her drawings,
each comes with a gasp and merriment, laughter.
Monte eavesdrops from the other end of the paint-
lavished studio; he caws, his song echoes on the wind.

Abstraction

I woke up this morning missing my heart. Apparently it was wrenched
from my chest like a loose bolt and taken into custody by the fur trapper
from Iron Horse Lake. I'm told he collects them like cut pelts—trophies
from the wilderness—and exhibits them next to the oak and ivory inlaid
gun rack hanging over his bed. He has quite the collection, each with
distinguishing properties and carefully labeled signatures. Mine reads:
1965, Sioux Girl with Pearl Scalp. The others are not so plain. He spends
weeks sharpening his knives against the tenderness of their nerves,
honing his craft for the thrill of pursuit, sharpening his sense of smell,
encroaching their territories, rooting out those damp caves where his
souvenirs sleep. When the hearts are gathered and each chamber bled out
and exposed, he makes a portrait of them, an installation for the throngs
of curious eyes—those hungry patrons of the arts, that marvel at the dark,
elusive canvases of the absurd.

Liminal

Heid E. Erdrich

Liminal

from Whitman

Try to imagine the elastic vision of a child
whose chalky gray sidewalk
and rusted swing-set meant the world.

The whole enchanting world in flakes
sifted from cheap metal chains to dress
what little snow's left on a certain part of one day.

The scant brown grass at snow's retreat—
a lovely world of moss, a valley for the little people.
A world that was so good to bring back life

from the breathless blank winter of the prairie.
And the treasure the snow showed:
Maple leaf glassed in ice, perfectly green still.

Cat-eye marbles encrusting the sandbox like jewels.
At season's edge what we find matters most:
We get back what is lost in flux.

Hard lesson yet, for a girl who grew up
leaning in the doorway,
yearning for waves so far from any shore.

eBay Bones

Her skull goes to the highest bidder.
How much would you give for a warrior head?
Hawaii's history for an ashtray?
She was not much older than me.
Woman of volcanic earth so rich she probably
eased into the loam like her shawl,
wrapped up warm for her final sleep.
They should have buried her more deeply.
Should have thought of science's creepy needs.
Should have known the web would one day
hold our dead in its sacred sites.
The grave may be a fine and secret place,
but kept a fine secret only for some.
Others are History. And History
must be brought to light—
in the flash of an empty eye socket.

Someone will pay for this.
Someone did.
Her ivory grin worth
less than human curiosity,
less than the rest of all humanity,
all humanity at rest
beneath us all.

Other People's Children

Other people's children we can't
quite fathom. Whether wafting
like fairies or torn with tantrum
or full-faced with milky sleep.
We either adore them or glance away
at the parents, bless them, thinking:
Better yours than mine.

Other people's children,
mysteries all of them: Buddhas beaming,
silly as all get out or blinking and serene.
What scares them, soothes them, stalls them?
Stricken by strangers' looks,
no matter how kindly meant or
surly, unruly, truly unknowable—
Except by experts whose care's
given each day like milk, like air,
given to other people's children.

To other people's children and our own:
our own, much needed, other mothers.

Deborah A. Miranda

Credo

I believe that the scent of ions bristles on the edge
of a thunderstorm, chemically alters our brain cells

like the breath of a passing god.
I believe that round, sage green hills trigger

the heartsongs of ancestors still dwelling
in the ridges of blue mountains.

I believe the liquid jungle cries of robins overflow
from ancient fountains of praise.

I don't believe in promises pulled from weeping children,
or lovers. I don't believe in the noble poor,

the noble savage, or the born-again politician.
I believe in a brilliant, distracted Creator

who's forgotten to feed the kids but snags
a Nobel with that terra cotta sculpture. I believe

in the languid lure of purple phlox on the road home,
forget-me-nots sprouting in abandoned yards,

the fervent green cries of a thousand acorns
all sprouting in love at once.

Ghost Road Song

   for my father, 11/19/1927–6/27/2009

I need a song.
I need a song like a river, cool and dark and wet,
like a battered old oak; gnarled bark,
bitter acorns,
a song like a dragonfly:
shimmer—hover—swerve—

like embers, too hot to touch.

I need a song like my father's hands:
scarred, callused, blunt,
a song like a wheel,
like June rain, seep of solstice,
tang of waking earth.

I need a song like a seed:
a hard and shiny promise,
a song like ashes:
gritty, fine, scattered;
a song like abalone, tough as stone,
smooth as a ripple at the edge of the bay.

I need a song so soft, it won't sting my wounds,
so true, no anger can blunt it,
so deep, no one can mine it.

I need a song with a heart wrapped in barbed wire.

I need a song that sheds no tears,
I need a song that sobs.
I need a song that skates along the edge of black ice,
howls with coyotes,
a song with a good set of lungs,
a song that won't give out, give up,
give in, give way:
I need a song with guts.

I need a song like lightning, just one blaze of insight.

I need a song like a hurricane,
spiraled winds of chaos,
a snake-charming song,
a bullshit-busting song,
a shut-up-and-listen-to-the-Creator song.

I need a song that rears its head up like a granite peak
and greets the eastern sky.

I need a song small enough to fit in my pocket,
big enough to wrap around
the wide shoulders of my grief,
a song with a melody like thunder,
chords that won't get lost,
rhythm that can't steal away.
I need a song that forgives me my lack of voice.

I need a song that forgives my lack of forgiveness.

I need a song so right
that the first note splinters me like crystal,
spits the shards out into the universe
like sleek seedlings of stars; yes,
that's the song
I need,

the song to accompany you
on your first steps
along the Milky Way,
that song with ragged edges,
a worn-out sun;
the song that lets a burnt red rim
slip away into the Pacific,
leaves my throat
healed at last.

Ishi at Large
a found poem

A lone whale,
with a voice unlike any other,
has been wandering

the Pacific for the past
12 years. Using signals
recorded by the US navy
to track submarines,
researchers traced

the movement of whales
in the Northern Pacific
and found that a lone whale
singing at a frequency

of around 52 hertz
has cruised the ocean since 1992.
Its calls, despite being clearly
those of a baleen,

do not match those of any
known species of whale,
which usually call
at frequencies of between

15 and 20 hertz.
The mammal does not follow
the migration patterns
of any other species either,

according to team leaders.
The calls of the whale,
which roams the ocean
every autumn and winter,

have deepened slightly
as a result of aging,
but are still
recognizable.

Reva "Mariah" S. Gover

A Single Note

In the end it doesn't really matter
whether you've changed—I have
I used to think I wanted fairytale
devotion—now I know it's bullshit

No sweetheart, not just you and your
yellow eyes or the hard edge of your
panic, seeking endless escape
in my body—something infinitely closer
my own forty-nine song

We all know that those glorious nights
only last the quickly disappearing hours
of darkness, too soon the sun rises,
gnats find the corners of our eyes,
chiggers bite our legs—thirst parches
scratchy throats driving us all home

So maybe I should have known that your
kisses, though sweet, would eventually
drive me to my knees—your tongue
choke and leave me to calculate
my desperation for one moment alone

I know you don't understand, lover—knew
before my resolve hardened like liquid
rock rising from the steam of my determination.
Worse yet, I know you struggle to believe
that before the burn
how could I have
ever loved you?

Strangely, I'll let that question just lay still
in this early morning heat—I have nowhere
to put it and I almost like this single note
straining to dance in the air—I know the answer.
It is your uncertainty you hear
as I begin singing again.

Molly McGlennen

Interwoven

At thirty months old a baby is exactly
one-half her adult height, you said—

so you taught her to measure up right
stand under a ruler
against the wall as you'd slate
her progression over the years

a trellis of penciled story
how one vine slowed for a year
then shot up crazily

knees aching at night in bed
taller than all the boys
a basketball always in hand.

She'd hold herself still
not to tangle or waver
a climber perching on delicate lattice
earth-green stem with spaded leaves
overgrowth on a smudged wall of time

you'd line the rows for her:
the days she cried, hating herself
and her hand-me-down boy-shoes
for the beginning of season

how you'd spend the night scrubbing
and bleaching the soles and laces,
all of the halves you'd complete
before she realized.

Joan Kane

Hyperboreal

Arnica nods heavy-headed on the bruised slope.
Peaks recede in all directions, in heat-haze,
Evening in my recollection.

The shield at my throat ornamental and worse.
We descended the gully thrummed into confusion
With the last snowmelt a tricklet into mud, ulterior—

One wolfbane bloom, iodine-hued, rising on its stalk
Into the luster of air: June really isn't June anymore,
Is it? A glacier's heart of milk loosed from a thousand

Summer days in extravagant succession,
From the back of my tongue, dexterous and sinister.

Syllabics

The sun made new again
Shadows of ice
As vertebrae cut through.

Beauty unlike a blown
Glass bird, patterns
Of fluted beads—instead

Silt or sand, or something
Fractured. A plain
Of grit, a sediment.

From the forest the wind
Had utterly
Transformed, a small nest thrown

Into the path intact—
Moose hair and moss.
In their blue and distant

Taper, you hold in poise
Mountains: upon
Stone upon stone.

Jennifer Elise Foerster

Leaving Tulsa

Once, there were coyotes, cardinals
in the cedar. We could cure amnesia
from the trees of our back forty acres.

Once, I drowned in a monsoon of frogs.
Grandpa said: it's a good thing, a promise
for a good crop. Grandma's perfect tomatoes.
Squash.

She taught us to shuck corn
while laughing, never spoke
about her childhood, whose faces
were in the gingerbread tins
stacked in the closet.

When she died, she was covered in a quilt
the Creek way. But I don't know the way
for this kind of burial: the vanishing
toads, thinning of pecan groves, peach trees
replaced by transplanted palm. The new neighbors
tossing clipped grass over our fence line
complaining to the city of our overgrown fields.

In the twilight, I see white cranes
lift from the pond. I turn a smooth stone
from the creases in my palm
          lay it among the reeds.

My grandfather was a truck driver,
retired to grow a garden in the back
of our Indian allotment land.
Grew watermelon. Took us grandkids fishing
for dragonflies. When the bulldozers came
unannounced, with their documents
from the city and a truckload of pipelines,
his shotgun was already loaded.

Red bricks under the bent chestnut:
the well where my great aunt's husband
stored his whiskey. Buried beneath the roots
her bundle of colored beads. *They tell the story
of our family—* Cosetta's land—
flattened to a parking lot, our cornfield
a cobweb of husks.

After the funeral, I stowed
her jewelry underground, promised to return
when the rivers rose.

Grandpa potted me a cedar sapling
to take on the road for luck.
He's using the bark for the lesions
over his heart that the doctors can't explain.
To him it is a map, traces of home
or the Milky Way, where he's going, he says.

What could y'all know of it?
What could you do with it if you did,
he asks. Some things are inevitable. The word *cancer*
is tangled in the broken barbed wire
that kept the cows in the pasture
before the pasture was sold.

On the grassy plain behind the house
one buffalo remains. A white
rose. White as the cranes. I am
reminded of my own body
as I pay the rising Creek Turnpike toll.

In the gravel pits along the highway
sunflowers stand in dense rows. Telephone poles
jut crookedly into the layered sky. A crow's beak
broken by a windmill's blade. And I finally understand
my grandpa when he says

he doesn't know how to stave 'em off much longer—
when they see open land,
they only know to take it. I understand

how to walk at sunset among the haybales
looking for turtle shells, how to sing
over the sound of the county road widening
to four lanes for commuter traffic, and I understand

how to keep from looking up—
small planes overhead must be tracking me
as I kneel in the Johnson grass
brushing away footprints.

Up here, parallel to the median
with a vista of mesas like crossknots of a weaving
the sky is a mosaic of blue and white beads.
In my rearview mirror I see
our 160-acre stamp on God's forsaken country:
a roof blown off a shed, beams bent like matchsticks,
a herd of white cows building their home
in a rusted derailed train car

and I imagine a land I come from still,
a pocket under roots to return to,
that I am not just another lost American
smashing butterflies on her windshield,
addicted to the open range and the highway
that crosses it like a perfectly straight seam
hemming up all the broken dreams
we come from.

Once, I thought trees were medicine for sleep.

Once, I thought her buried beads
could tell the story for me.

Once, I dreamt of inheriting
my mother who still follows
the larks through the field,
my sister's small hand
tucked inside hers, me on her breast
in the burial quilt.

Jace DeCory

Sam, I Am

Received the news today—diagnosed with diabetes.
Strange that no one in the family has this disease.
No problem—will stay alive with insulin.

Received the news today—cancer has struck.
Mom and Dad died from this, yet remained strong to the end.
No problem—will take radiation and chemo to live.

Woke up today—couldn't walk or talk that well.
Mind tells my body to work, it has other thoughts.
No problem—will work to walk and talk again.

Pain in my legs today—they sometimes feel like clubs.
Many hours at the V.A. hospital—time to think,
About how these strong legs took me through the jungles and the highlands.
No problem—will train my legs to handle the poor circulation and neuropathy.

Back hurts today—too many jumps and hard landings.
Crushed lower disks, can't walk too far, can't sit too long
No problem—must eat the pain.

Heard the news today—kidneys are shot.
First an access in the neck and a permanent one in the arm.
No problem—will take the "oil changes" to live.
Have the hours now to think and pray.

Started the day today—burning and rash the shape of a ruck sack on my back.
Subsiding for awhile, but returning with fervor.
After all these years, still comes back.
No problem—break the bumps and dry with alcohol.

Received the news today—a leg must go.
Agent Orange, how insidious at first.
Still smell the jungle burning.
No problem—cut off the pain, and live another day.

Gordon D. Henry

Sonny's Wake 2000

After Joe Bush prays
With the bear pwaagun
After Swan and the boys
From Pine Point make
The vocal ascension
To sing some honor song

Wandering children hear
This school's janitor ghost
In the hallways
During the catholic liturgy.

We all pass
The floral presentations
The messages of regret
The army decorations
A golden gloves fight card
The arrangements of photos
The last of a thinner man
His foot on the front bumper
Of a red galaxy

Ahead of us a few
Of the old ones—
leech lake hymn
singers—genuflect,
then kneel.
Steady eyed before
The silver casket
They whisper so
Softly the movement
Of our skin
In our best clothes
Is all we hear.

Ralph Salisbury

Some Hunts

A hunter climbing a deer trail,
shale slipping, recalls
calves sizzling in the barn
burned down, some lightning bolts ago,
foundation stones, laid by his granddad, a bed
for kittens' skeletal huddle, as intricate
as his mother's tatted antimacassar.

Bone hands try
to set table with service he threw
on the junk pile, crazed, after World War Two
discarded so much.

Heart failing, sixty some years,
of appetite, turned into prayer,
venison starts feet stalking up a trail and, moss
under loose shale shifting, he leaps
to the next uncertainty.

Living in the Mouth

Its strainers just wide enough
to gulp minuscule krill,
a baleen whale spits Jo-
nah, syl-
lable on syl-
lable, into preachers' unbelievers' ears,
and teaches humanity humility.

On photo paper, arms hold
some loved ones' years—of war after war—but,
another grandchild soon to be born, I foretell
temporal sensations' lovely creations and hope to live on,
until all of my tellings and foretellings become
the prairies and trees,
in Passenger Pigeons' songs

The Child, The War

A nun's wimpled collar, a cloud, becomes,

with sundown, after news
of my playmate's soldier daughter, the slash
around the throat of a pet pig,

whose sandpaper ears a child could reach over a fence
and stroke without
the gluey rubber snout and rusted crooked spike teeth's
reaching him,
then

Or None

The landlord's refuse-can's
hinges are squeaking like geriatric mice,
and my ageing aching body's door
to a shower's my own ghost,
complaining that I did not die young.

These years, when
there's more to remember than
to live, I am recollecting the war:

my mind's eighteen years:
some rooms, with no ceilings and
with floors which did not creak,
despite combat boots and slender slippers,
my fingers, newly adept with flesh's
mysteries, training to take
machine guns apart so many times
they came to seem, themselves, just mechanisms,
in darkness which is,
as I remember a bomber's uncertain flight, the sky—
ahead: an unlighted landing-strip, or none.

Travis Hedge Coke

Impromptu 49er, 1:25 a.m. in Los Angeles

The street comes up under your feet because it loves you:

> it's a graduated walk
> comfortably curbside, under
> glass, neon, and night.

Moths hit streetlamps through rain, mapping stars with their wounds:

> step between cars generating
> syncopated breaths in
> the vacuum of their speed.

Shae's hooking it on Broadway and Seventh, or just waiting for the light
to change:

> chance encounter, we say hi
> 'cause it's always colder after
> you pass somebody up, innit?

It's a longer walk knowing we'll u-turn it soon, but I keep my cash in my
sock and you closer:

> three coffees come fast
> from an all night diner
> lukewarm in tall Styrofoam.

I always edge the curb on return trips, somehow trying not to fall into
the street:

> warmer inside with you
> but I can't make someone wait
> out in the cold like that.

There is a symmetry in the arrangement of streets, like a love letter:

> I give Shae a coffee under the light
> same reason I gave you one; tradition
> not expecting you to get me back.

You only ever see returns if you're coming back this way.

sharing on the outer banks

do you dream in rooms
familiar from you
and do you dream
of doors where there never
were doors
do you
know who waits
standing behind
the walls in your
dreams

on the outer banks with the dead
i am drinking tea under clouds
like an open pomegranate

i split my roll as i write this
and halve my tea into two
cups, tell a story to the dead
on the banks of the waters of concern,
writing this not in trade
not in debt or necromancy, nothing
fancy like that, sharing tea and a story

i split my role as i right
corrections on the banks shoals
in the small afterlife town

Old Frost

Dust on the neck
Neck of a dead
Dust coats the feathers, tiny temperate feathers
On the neck
Of the winter of the decade
Decadent dents in the the the

Layli Long Soldier

Burial Flight
for Mark Turcotte

Stillborn   rocked on   father's chest   a house

     wood slats   unborn the   un-lips like   blue cracks

       cord bed   flesh room wet

    good God   the father   the pull   his head

a window   water streaks how   birds he thinks

    circle him in   approach retreat   a thousand count
                                      blood wings yank

an un-lung song   loadstone call   *Daddy Dad Father Pa*

snow face   sunken roof the   red white lights   in corners the walls

   blink spin   father to mother   one to un-other

        paper piles   wind house now

a drip leak God   each drop a head   like the unforeseen like

   a boy's hand   the could-bes   the *look Daddy look*

his crayon tips   could draw press   could each sharp V

                          two down stroke wings

could child a boy   could scrap paper

could black   and black could   those birds again

this man   stomach his gut   like you Mama feels

every kick jab   a buckshot blow   there the middle

center and parts   scatter   mad flying

or sometimes smaller   a bird   feet curled

bent branch   twig lift   quick flight   the rush

one to the greater   a speck flock how   the whole body rises

dives shifts   in cradle sky   this man   his chest

sways and rocks   it's in him   it's what   does not happen.

Dilate

I

Placed

on my chest   warm fragile

as the skin of nightfall she was   heavier than imagined   her eyes

untied from northern poles from   hard unseen   winter months

she arrived safely   mid-Spring she   scrunched her brow

an up-look   to her father. There's a turning   as pupils dilate

as black, vernal suns slip   into equinox. This was

we never forget her

first act.

II

All is experienced

throu

g

h

the

body,

somebody told me.

III

Though I did not feel it

when the mid-wife invited   when he cut   the tie

the clean   umbilical sever when   I smiled I did   not feel it

as they took her   to wash to weigh her   when I said

you should go with her.

Both of them gone   father and baby

in the room in warm   orange light   I listened from behind

a clock on the wall   my own face   heavy plate glass

though all experience

is ~~through~~ the body   I did not feel my

hands pull   white sheets my legs shake when   two nurses cooed

lean back   honey you are   bleeding more than expected.

Wakalyapi

1. a word commonly used for coffee;
2. formally meaning anything that is boiled. As in to boil the white collars, to boil the stiff in need of less hardening. As in the day, as it blows, will boil stiff trees. As in the boiling blood, what was not soft, traces a way through muscle to face. As in the muscle that is boiled away from the gristle. As in the pot, with the white collars and gristle. As in a boiling pot over which you are bent, you are watching. As in it will stir in your head as roots of a tree. As in the tree beneath which you left something buried. As it preferred to be buried than the fury of boiling. Or the rabbit they caught, the rabbit they boiled. As in the rabbit that came nightly, the jaw of your yard. As in the dinner you ate, the rabbit bone gnawed. As in the boiling blood you never do see. As in oleanders grown over a chain link fence, where roots of a tree and oleander mix. Boiled and boiled in a stew, the collars and rabbits and forts in a tree. As in the rabbit in a cage outside in the sun. As in the heat, as it boiled the rabbit was dead. As in the checks and bank statements momma boiled in the kitchen. As in the riddance of debt; a ceremony, a boiling. As in money was numbers, we would eat and not waste. As in two rabbits you remember boiled that summer: one who was caught, the other helpless in black fur—as your black pet rabbit you forgot to move to the shade. As in you cried in your room child, how could you forget. As in the shade that was grace that was oleander waves. As in the bubbles in water, what comes from this boiling. As something so light, now bloodless beneath.

Diane Glancy

Flight #4415

Birds are trouble.
You've sworn you won't fly with them again.
Turn the bones of their wings into pages of a flight log.
You say the plane is slow.
The pilots still on their way to the airport
long after departure time.
They send you messages. They arrive in chirps.
But they are flying now.
The cloud cover is below you.
The top of compacted clouds are feathers as if a white bird over the world.
They don't say where they've been but fly south
the way they've always heard.

Chicken Wife

> He won't look at no one. He just sits there like a stump.
> I have to go out and talk to the chickens.
> —Mary Benson c. 1923

He dreams of animals—Wolf. Otter. Fox. Snake. It was a bear I think
clawed a tree until the people came out. They were supposed to be
brothers, but got to fighting. There was no way to put the people back into
the tree. A dream comes roostering him here and there. My husband just
stares at the wall. How can he be awake while he dreams? His father and
grandfather were sachems who saw the what was coming as if already
here. My father never let me go hungry. My father talked to me. He took
me fishing. My father had a deer-hide map marked with boundaries, paths
and rivers—Salamonie. Tippecanoe. Wabash. Sangamon. I put my finger
in the arrow hole in the hide. It was over 100 years old. The hens fight
over one grain. We have to clear out and make room for others, my father
said. We're on our way to another place. He left when I was married. If
my husband's dreams come in planting or harvest, I have it all by myself.
When Jess was old enough he'd hold the bucket. But his sisters nagged

him to play or taunted him. I thought sometimes the children would peck one another to death. Them hens always looking on the ground as if a fox wasn't in the woods. As if as if my rifle was on the porch. In the Bible*—Jesus went out of the house and sat by the sea. A multitude followed, looking for their grain. Clucking in their sandals, their great toes like claws. I tie a twig of vine on my head for the comb chickens wear. Cluck. Cluck. I talk to the hens in their language—How you doing? Heard from the children? Think those storm clouds'll pass? BUCK, BUCK, I say. My husband's a sachem instead of a husband. The terrible wilderness is howling. The vipers and scorpions got us in their sight. I gather acorns to grind for flour, leaching the acid from them. I cook porridge with heated rocks in a coiled basket and set it on the stoop for my husband, but he won't eat when he's dreaming. A sour man with a yellow-green face lurks near the trees. I throw a heated rock at him. You hens on your perches at night, what do you dream? You cackle as if on fire. One eye waking. In the other eye a dream. Those little red flames on your heads.

*Matthew 13:1

Laura Tohe

blue book #5

half of your moon hangs on your side of the world

      mine hangs outside my bedroom window

where the cicadas sing the last of their summer songs

      in the desert night

soon they will sing us into   another season then leave us

and I will be left to make my way and you yours

where are the billie holiday songs that will

         lift the heavy boot of our longing?

and where is the poetry to soothe our hurting hearts?

yours grew wings and flew across the ocean like a butterfly

blue book #6

is she a slut?

the woman who goes to bed with whomever

she feels the heat with

or is she only a woman with many lovers

who want only to kiss her fingertips,

read her ferlinghetti,

and touch her hair?

Activist

rushing
    toward the mountains
  of flesh and water
    it lifts itself
      departs from the body
  drifts above the pines,
    canyon walls and temporal creations of a steely world
like mist it floats
      with breath of mountain
and what happens then?
    a rush to the north?
  a four day journey to the places of maternal love?
    to the land your ancestors found agreement with?
  linger in the arms of the male mountain
    you sacrificed yourself for?
  you are the blood-soul of the ancients
    who know the language of plants and old pines
  you, who has seen beauty in the things unseen

Jon Henson

To Grow Older

As you grow older
A deeper understanding
      of the world creeps upon you
To be able to understand the simplest times

Preparing to cook dinner
      meat seasoned awaiting heat

Sitting at the kitchen table
      enjoying the warmth of the woodstove

The cold february wind blowing
      outside
Sunset over the la platas

Smells of burnt cedar
      from my small cast iron skillet

This is a pure time
Void of colonial america
A simple time permanently fixed

Just waiting to start dinner
      not thinking of war
            peace

Just enjoying this time—

By the River in Winter

River
        partially frozen
Holding the spirit
        of summer with the crystals

A bald eagle perched
        in the skeletal remains
            of a tree

Watching water flow by
        attempting to touch the same water
            twice

All I achieved was getting wet—

Roberta J. Hill

After the War, the Head Nurse Gives Advice to Wives Visiting the Ward

The man inside the man
closed himself in a cave.
His safety's a secretion. Don't shells
cover up the terror
of being soft? Mollusks evolved
long before men. Yes, it's a return and we
call it 'regression.'
His defenses got him ill. A spiraling
down until he was a shell person
burlesquing bits of
adaptations, accommodations, miming
a frown or smile as infants do.

The man inside the man held through
church and school erasing his spirit, through
the winding sheets of commerce,
through the horrors of war and torture.
His shell protected him
but grew on trauma until in a
sudden pinch
he laughed and began
to split.

So, accept it, Mrs. Powell, Mrs. Ash.
The man inside the man
can't love you now. He says it, but
some cover is needed, no? If you want
him whole, he needs your loving gaze.
I wrote my thesis on the true gaze that
helps the star-born spirits that we are
descend again into our groins.

Yes, Mrs. Burl, that is
another visit. Your man now needs
you to accept how he'll
evade or lie, trip you so you

deny the truth of the man inside
the man. The pain he buried
forces him to divide his brain
until he's like confetti. He
sees his own hand with its grooved
prints alien as a fork as that hand reaches
for a door on a clattering train
and once inside a seat, he's still not
safe. So the division repeats, repeats,
repeats until, by the time you reach him,
he's a million men, shoulder
to shoulder marching to
a fascist tune.

The man inside the man
gets hard to find in that melee.
Believe your love
strong enough to get through this?

Inside him millions hug their guns,
make speeches on loudspeakers while
flags wave, eyeballs lock on sights, plans
for world domination on the route where
another million die dammed as
the multitudes mount their missiles.
If you love enough, you will sacrifice
what you expect to see in order
to watch those millions march while
the man inside spins eight inches
above his own left ear. Oh, you say,
he's solid as a wrestler. Did you protest
the war or let it slide along, thinking
in one month it would be over?

Inside
he's swept by millions

at quark speed and is quitting life
just as fast. How paradoxical
to learn from this ward how
much humanity can't be alone. We live
because we're loved.
Please! Put away
that phone. Now, you mustn't say
"I see you." He'll hold back until you leave
then fragment
even more. War goes on even after
men come home. So, choose to ignore
his fragments and touch his elbow,
not with a grip, but lightly, as if two electric
currents passed to become a glowing bulb.
He'll resist, cringe at being seen,
banter to persuade you all to leave,
but touch and song the only way
to coax his spirit down from the sky
to find his hair. Once it's there, rub
his back and keep your loving light.
You can also sing. Singing gets rid
of many things.

How sad
the State cut out songs and dreams.
How odd to tell you now—
keep faith with water
so you can accept all
the many ways he'll try to drown.

Lance Henson

Poem from Amman

Too far the jester whispered as I landed from Bavaria
How far is that I wrote on the dust on the table
The dragon lady with a dark pen scribbling my face
On the desert wind

And all the words I used on the telephone
Could not spell your name

Eating meat on a road near the airport
Under the pleiades
Desert cops with friendly guns arrived
Shook hands and drove off
Toward the war inside their minds

Seven dogs in mythic masks appeared from a sacred hole
In the universe
The two that would not leave are with me now
Their eyes shine in the rains that hover over the human
Shit storm

A glistening night keeps falling out of my head

Moonlight shining on the tobacco prayers
Under the tomb
Of a fallen king. . . .

Lois Beardslee

Manitogiizans/December

When I asked my mother
If she could remember
What her mother's mother called December
Before the Black-Robed religious reformers
Named it LittleSpiritMoon
After their BabyJesus

She put her open hand
To her own lips
Shook her head
Looked away
Said we are better off
If we do not remember those things.

Ñeñe'i Ha-ṣa:gid

(In the Midst of Songs)

Joy Harjo

Eagle Song

To pray you open your whole self
To sky, to earth, to sun, to moon
To one whole voice that is you
And know there is more
That you can't see, can't hear
Can't know except in moments
Steadily growing, and in languages
That aren't always sound but other
Circles of motion.
Like eagle that Sunday morning
Over Salt River. Circled in blue sky
In wind, swept our hearts clean
With sacred wings.
We see you, see ourselves and know
That we must take the utmost care
And kindness in all things.
Breathe in, knowing we are made of
All this, and breathe, knowing
We are truly blessed because we
Were born, and die soon within a
True circle of motion,
Like eagle rounding out the morning
Inside us.
We pray that it will be done
In beauty.
In beauty.

Ofelia Zepeda

Ñeñe'i Ha-ṣa:gid

Ha-ka: 'ac g ñeñei'i mo 'am kaidaghim
'Am kaidaghim taṣ huḍñig wui.
'Am kaidaghim si'alig ta:gio.
'Am kaidaghim ju:pin ta:gio.
'Am kaidaghim wakolim ta:gio.
'Am 'ac ha'icug 'id ṣa:gid.
mo 'am kaidaghim
S-ap ta:hadag 'o g t-i:bdag.
S-ape 'o g t-cegĭtodag.
S-ape 'o g t-jewedga.
S-ke:kaj 'o, ñia 'an g 'i-ñeid.
S-ju:jpig 'o, ñia 'an g 'i-ñeid.

Ka: 'ac g ka:cim ṣu:dagi t-miabĭ 'at.
Ka: 'ac g ge'e jegos t-miabĭ 'at.
Ka: 'ac g ṣ -ke:g hewel t-miabĭ 'at.
Ka: 'ac g ṣ -ke:g ñeñe' t-miabĭ 'at.
Ka: 'ac g ṣ -ke:g ñeñe't-ai 'at.

In the Midst of Songs

We hear the songs resounding.
They are resounding toward the sunset.
They are resounding toward the sunrise.
They are resounding toward the north.
They are resounding toward the south.
We are in the midst of songs.
Our heart is full of joy.
Our mind is good.
Our land is good.
The land is all beautiful, take a look.
There is light rain all around, take a look.

We hear the ocean in the distance.
It has come near us.
We hear the beautiful wind in the distance.
It has come near us.
We hear the dust storm in the distance.
It has come near us.

We hear a beautiful song in the distance.
It has come near us.
We hear a beautiful song in the distance.
It has come upon us.

Jeweḍ 'I-hoi

Kuṣ haṣcu hab a:g mat hab o cei
"an ep ta:tk mat si i-hoi g jeweḍ
Nap pi ṣa'i ta:tk a:pi?"
Pi'a, pi'a.
Kuṣ haṣcu hab a:g?
Kutp hemps heg hab a:g mat o ṣa e-hai g jeweḍ k o i-hoi
A no heg hab a:g mat sikol o memḍad mo g milga:n b a'a' 'rotation'
Ñia, kutp hems heg hab a:g mo hegai ta:tk
Kutp hems hab e-elid mo an ke:d 'id jeweḍ da:m c da'a an da:m kacim
    Oidc
Ceṣṣajcuk g jeweḍ
masma mat hemakc g ṣ-melidkam kawyu o ceṣṣacug
An medad c g mo'oj ṣelim an e-widut huhu'u mehidag ku:bṣ oidc
    ṣ-ke:g hab ma:ṣ
Heg an we:maj wiappoi mo an ko:mcugg taṣ c gahŭ amjed i-bebhĕ
Si'alig ta:gio amjed gamhu hukkam hudñig ta:gio
Ñia, kut hegai maṣ d maṣad ced o'odham o si al hehemaḍ matṣ an o bij

Earth Movement

She said she felt the earth move again
I never knew whether she meant she felt a tremor
Or whether it was the rotation of the earth.
I like to think she felt the rotation, because anyone can feel a tremor.
And when she felt this
She could see herself standing on the earth's surface
Her thick wide feet solidly planted
Toes digging in
Her visualization so strong
She can almost feel her body arch against the centrifugal force of the
        rotation
She can see herself with her long hair floating
Floating in the atmosphere of stardust
She rides her planet the way a child rides a toy
Her company is the boy who takes the sun on its daily journey
And the man in the moon smiles as she passes by.

Okokoi

D 'o si we:pegkam
D 'o siwepegkam
Hegai mo añ je:ek
G ṣ-ke:g bahidaj
Ñi'a, ñi'a
ṣ-wa'usim cewagi 'o i:bhe

Mourning Dove

She is the first one
She is the first one
Who tastes
the beautiful fruit
See here, see here
She breathes clouds of wetness.

Jorge Miguel Cocom Pech

Fragmentos del Libro Inédito
El Chilam Balam de Calkiní

1

Tumen pek' mina'an u k'abo'ob,
ku toojol ch'íibal
ti'a'al u ch'ínik u k'uxil.

2

Uuje'
jach chunpaja'an u wíinbail
kan u lúusik u nóok'e'
ku sut'kuba siip'a'an poolyíim
ku t'abik k'ak'il tsuum in kibe'
ku jum yáanal in tuch.

3

U yáawatil pek'
ti'a'al chí'íibal u jaats' nóok'íl ak'abe'.

4

T'aané,
wa yant'íi,
jump'éel kuuchil tu'ux ku líisiij nok,
mi bin je u táakik u bóonil ch'ench'enki'o'ob.

5

Táak'antal íiche'
u ch'uujuk yich kuulché.
Ma'a tun ts'o'k a t'ookik yéetel a jáantik:
ts'o'ok u lúuk'ech yéetel u bóonil u paakat'.

6

Míise'
kan u p'oík u wíinklil chuumuk na'e,
tan u ya'ik tech:
yan bin u k'uchul maak,
ma'a a wóoje'tu taal u lak'intkech.

Le beetiké,
kan u séebil u yichkí tu táanil a uich
ku yéeesik tech ti'i u k'a'k'il u yíiché
ti'a'an u yíichil a wóotoché
ku páaktik'o'b ba'al bin kun úuchukí.

Fragmentos del Libro Inédito
El Chilam Balam de Calkiní

1

Porque el perro carece de manos,
ladra para arrojar sus enojos.

2

La luna,
completamente llena
al desnudarse,
se trastoca en hinchado pezón,
que enciende la mecha
que crepita debajo de mi ombligo.

3

El aullido de un perro,
es su forma de morder los harapos de la noche.

4

La palabra,
si tuviera un ropero,
guardaría el color de los silencios.

5

La fruta madura,
es el ojo dulce de un árbol.
Antes de que la cortes y la comas:
te ha devorado con el color de su mirada

6

El gato,
cuando en medio de la casa lava su cuerpo,
dice que habrá visita inesperada.
Por eso,
cuando aprisa se baña delante de ti,
te muestra que el fuego de sus ojos,
son los ojos de tu casa que miran el futuro.

Fragments from the unedited book
   The Chilam Balam of Calkiní

1

Because the dog lacks hands,
he barks to throw his anger.

2

The moon,
completely full
while undressing,
disarranges herself in swollen nipple
that lights up the fuse
that crackles under my navel.

3

A dog's howl,
is his way of biting the night's tatters.

4

The Word,
if it had a wardrobe,
Would keep the color of silences.

5

The ripe fruit,
is the sweet eye of a tree.
Before you pick and eat it:
it has devoured you with the color of its glance.

6

The cat,
when in the middle of the house washes his body,
says there will be an unexpected visit.
Thus,
when hurriedly he washes in front of you,
he shows that his eyes' fire,
are the eyes of your house watching the future.

translated from Mayan and Spanish by Juan Nevarez

El niño maestro

¡Señor!
No necesitas ser adulto para enseñar.
Oculto en la sutil sonrisa de mi alumno, estás tú.

Si algo me aflije,
si mi corazón recibe la visita de las abrojos,
él,
provisto de tu sabiduría,
intenta atrapar mis cuitas con sus preguntas

Y se las lleva al patio de los juegos.
Y ahí, (OJO)
recluidas en el vientre de un Viejo balón:
de pie en pie,
de pase en pase,
hecha trizas por el griterío y la ovación convulsa,
mis cuitas,
sucumben aprisionadas en las redes de la portería.

¡Señor!
No necesitas ser adulto para enseñar.
Oculto en la sutil sonrisa de mi alumno, estás tú.

The Kid Teacher

God!
You don't need to be an adult to teach.
Hidden in my pupil's subtle smile, there you are.

If something makes me upset,
if my heart is visited by thorns,
he,
provided with your wisdom,
traps my troubles with the flapping of their questions.

And he takes them to the playground,
and there,
imprisoned in the belly of an old ball,
from foot to foot,
from pass to pass,
shattered by the shouting and the agitated ovation,
(my troubles)
they succumb trapped in the goalkeeper's nets.

God!
You don't need to be an adult to teach.
Hidden in my pupil's subtle smile, there you are.

translated from Spanish by the author

Hugo Jamioy

Aty Tima Zarkuney, At¨sbe Buiñent¨san Onÿnaná

(Juahscon buashinÿinÿanbe Mamá)

At¨sbe Bembbiam

Chëté sënján tëjaján
chë tanguá niñë¨sëng
chë celoca orquideushangá jtsaitëmiám
nÿe canÿeshá
nderado,
at¨sbiam enjobatmán
jinÿinÿiyám cabá nduant¨sefjon or
acbe bominÿ;
chë mallajt betiyëng tejan tsoyn
chë versiay shloft¨s enjetsichamo;
cháendmën, chë cachent¨sa betiyent¨sán onÿnaná
cochtsábobiamnay
yëbsán chaunt¨sefjonam.

Tima Aty Zarkuney, brote de mi sangre

(Tima Aty Zarkuney, Madre de la Fertilidad de la Luna)

A mi hija

Aquel día caminé por el monte
los leños viejos
escondían las orquídeas en el cielo
solo una,
esperaba mi visita
para mostrarme en sus bellos colores
tus ojos;
mas al fondo de la espesa montaña
el pájaro cantor decía:
ella, es el brote de una planta de esta tierra
abónala,
para que mañana florezca.

Tima Aty Zarkuney, Flow of My Blood

(Tima Aty Zarkuney, Fertility Mother of the Moon)

for my daughter

That day I walked the wild
Ancient tree stumps
Hid the sky orchids
Only one
Waited for my visit
So as to display in its luminous colors
Your eyes
Further into the deep of the thick mountain
The song bird said:
She, is the flow of a plant of this earth
Nourish her
Tomorrow she will blossom.

translated from Kamsa and Spanish by Juan Felipe Herrera

Espej Ca Inÿna Yomn Ndegombr Soy

Teojtsenoshecy ingacá
cat¨sbet ibet tojtsemna or
jeninÿenam contsobecocná
chë nt¨sam yomncá espejoc
chabe jobiañ ndoñ quenatsbomn lunarëng juinÿnanam
cha echandbetsan y mo ftsestoncá cmochantsibión;
cochanjobatm acbe yebnoc
cochantsentënÿay ibetoy jobuertanam
canÿe té masque cochantsebo¨s
ndoñ quecochatobenay acbe benach jajbanan
cha cmochantsobatmán
chacotsëstonam
as cochanjinÿ acbe cuerp espejcá inyná yomna.

Plateada es la realidad

Cada paso que das
en la noche de luna llena
te acerca al encuentro
con el espejo plateado de la realidad;
en su rostro no tiene lunares que la marquen
ella camina y sientes que te persigue;
detienes los pasos en tu choza
evitando dar el giro de la oscuridad;
algún día, aunque tú quieras
no podrás detener tu camino
ella te estará esperando
para que sigas sus pasos
y verás que tu cuerpo es plateado en realidad.

Silvery Is Reality

Every step that you take
On a full moon night
Pulls you to the encounter
with the slivery mirror of reality
On her countenance there are no dark growths that mark her
She ambles only and you sense her pursuit;
Your footsteps stutter by your hut
Avoiding to whirl darkness;
One day, even against your will
You will not be able to force back your path
She shall be waiting
For you to follow her footsteps
And you will notice your body silvery in the reality.

translated from Kamsa and Spanish by Juan Felipe Herrera

Shinÿ y juashcón

Chë shinÿ basetem tonjebtsotëjajo
juashcon jishacham entsebo¨s;

chë juashcón basetem oyejuayá entsoboyejuá
shinÿbe buacuajënguent¨san entsachán;

inÿe or chabe mamá (Tsbatsana Mamá)
bochanjuauyaná chë jeninÿenama or
quenatsbo¨s chabe bemb chamotsambañam
er canÿa nanjoqueda ibetë¨siñ.

Eclipse

El niño sol corre adolescente
quiere alcanzar a la luna;

la niña luna danza coqueta
esquiva los brazos del sol;

a veces, su madre
se entromete en sus encuentros
no quiere que se lleven a su hija
se quedará sola en la oscuridad.

Eclipse

The child-sun skitters adolescent
It desires to touch the moon;

The moon-girl sways and flirts
Shy she dodges the sun's embraces;

At times, her mother
Jumps into the fray of her encounters
She does not want her daughter to be taken

She will remain alone in the darkness.

translated from Kamsa and Spanish by Juan Felipe Herrera

Shecuat¨sëng Bet¨sa¨soc

T¨sabá namna
shecuat¨seng, bet¨sa¨soc jtsebomnán,
at¨sbe Taitá, echandbayan,
ndocnaté jtanëngcá chacotsnam.

Los Pies En La Cabeza

Siempre es bueno
tener los pies en la cabeza,
dice mi taita,
para que tus pasos nunca sean ciegos.

The Feet on the Head

It is always good
To have the feet on the head,
My taita says,
So your footsteps shall never go blind.

translated from Kamsa and Spanish by Juan Felipe Herrera

Tonday chiatayán, nÿe sënjenojuabó

Taitábe uchanëshañ chë plumushangac
sënjenojuabó, botaman shloft¨s tojobaniyec;
chë Taitá, at¨sbent¨san bënoc endanan
tonjobeconá y ¨sonjauyán:
at¨s ndoñ cheyatóba.
sënjonÿen tsenëguëngbe luaroc
jtsetat¨sëmbuam nt¨sam bejuabnayan.
Chent¨sán tontsatoñ.

No dije nada, solo pensé

Esas plumas que lleva el Taita en su corona
me hicieron pensar en la muerte de un guacamayo;
el Taita que caminaba distante de mi
se acercó y me dijo:
yo no lo maté
lo recogí en el salado de los loros
fue mi ofrenda
para adquirir el poder de adivinar el pensamiento;
luego se marchó.

I Did Not Say Anything, Just Thought

Those feathers that the Taita carries on his head
Made me think about the death of the guacamayo bird;
The Taita that ambled ahead of me
Approached me and said:
I did not kill it
I found it in the place of the singing birds
It was my offering
To acquire the power of divining:
Then he walked away.

translated from Kamsa and Spanish by Juan Felipe Herrera

Al Hunter

A Secret of Birds

I wanted to kiss you

To reach out and gently cup your face
And will you

Past our unspoken pause of years
Within our closing gyre
Our widening desire
As the years encircle us

For years, like birds, we rode imperceptible kettles of wind
Aloft and soaring
Sometimes pulled nearer
On subtle swoops and fly-bys
A sky dance of wind and wings
Sometimes pulled afar
In migrations that followed separate stars and constellations
Only to migrate here again
Softly singing memory songs of return and longing

Finally, aloft of our unspoken pause of years
Finally, reaching across feather-light and closing the distance
Your face gently cupped in wings
Desire fluttered and hovered—hesitation
We alight softly together, we . . .
Finally, ah . . . your mouth, your mouth, your lips, ever so slightly parted
Finally, yes . . . my mouth, on your mouth, our lips parting softly . . .
Again, yes, yes again . . . please . . . again
Slowly, tenderly we press our mouths together
Yes, tenderly, like hungry, hesitant birds
Wanting to linger, lest it be our one and only, our last
And then, then,
To take wing, to take wing,
And soar . . .

Lacuna

In the hollows between time and forgiveness
In between love and longing.
In the hollows between grace and faith
In between diamonds and the rough.
In the hollows between struggle and freedom
In between flotsam and pearls.
In the hollows between earth and sky
In between anguish and recovery.
In the hollows between darkness and dawn
In between memory and healing.
In the hollows between proof and promises
In the hollows between love and loss
Finding you.

Winter Birds

Some winter birds
Scrabble in the waning light of short days
That disappears with the sun
Out of reach of furtive eyes
And wings.

Some winter birds
Scrabble in the starling
That disappears in the snow
Out of reach of beaks
And talons.

Some winter birds
Scrabble in the moonlight
That disappears beyond the trees
Out of reach of flight
And season.

Some winter birds
Scrabble for orientation and order
That disappears in the darkness
Out of reach of desire
And reason.

Some winter birds
Scrabble for directions and association
That disappears in the mire
Out of reach of dreams
And vision.

Radiance, warmth and illumination
As elusive as the waning light in the short days of winter
As elusive as starlight in the snow
As moonlight beyond the trees
As elusive as direction and association
As elusive as winter birds on light wings.

Out of the Gallows

gossamer threads keep me here
dancing at the edge of grandeur
wobbly faith woven into a precarious grace
gossamer threads keep me here
bound to this earth
this lucid sphere

ragged threads keep me here
dangling at the edge of darkness
between subjugation
and a dark-hooded stranger
ragged threads keep me here
bound to this hell
this tattered diaphone

bound to this earth
this earth
gossamer threads keep me here
keep me
keep me
keep me here
bound to this earth
this earth
this earth
this earth

Jack D. Forbes

Weenoway-Okaan

Mohoomsena
Geeshaylaymokon
Nooweenoway
Weechemeenen
Kweenonokook koxweesak
Waymee aawinhaakay-ok
Kweenonokook koxweesak

Weenoway-yok
Weenoway-yok
Waymee hitkook
Kweenonokook koxweesak

Weenoway-yok
Weenoway-yok
Waymee awenik
Kweenonokook koxweesak

Begging

Grandfather
Grandfather of us all
Creator of us all
I am begging
Help all of us
Begging of you, your grandchildren
Every Native person
Begging of you, your grandchildren

They are begging
They are begging
Every tree
Begging of you, your grandchildren

They are begging
They are begging
Every creature
Begging of you, your grandchildren

> translated from Lenape by the author

Naaga Elkee

Naaga elkee
Naaga elkee
Guntka ok daasooee

Naaga elkee
Naaga elkee
Guntkay ok aasool

In a Little While

In a little while
In a little while
I will dance and sing

In a little while
In a little while
You will dance and sing

> translated from Lenape by the author

Opan

Yookway mechee opan
Yookway
Nuweekweehila
Kweekweehilaahech?
Delemee gaas-tong-aam!
Neechoos
Alamee gaas-tong-aam
Neechoos
Maacheetoom

Dawn

Now it is dawn
Now
I am tired
Are you tired?
I am sleepy!
My girlfriend
You are sleepy
My girlfriend
Let's go home

translated from Lenape by the author

Fredy Romeiro Campo Chicangana

Danza De Amor

En silencio acudo a tu cita
Llego a la orilla del río plateado
Y espero
La luna amarilla me mira tímidamente
Desde la otra orilla
Mi Corazón palpita bajo el cielo gris
No te veo, pero oigo tus pasos
Tus cantos de amor
Depronto apareces rompiendo el silencio
Y tocas el agua que se encharca en mi ser
Llegas y danzas para mis ojos
Entonces te tomo en mis brazos
y me fundo en un baile de amor
hay un encuentro que nos da la luz
el amor entre poeta y grulla

el canto que trae palabras secretas
vuelos, silencios, colores eternos . . .

Dance Of Love

In silence I come for your appointment
I arrive at the shore of the silver river
And wait
The yellow moon watches me timidly
From the other shore
My heart beats beneath the gray sky
I do not see you, but I hear your steps
Your songs of love
All at once you appear, breaking the silence
Touching the water that pools in my being

You arrive and dance for my eyes
Then I take you in my arms
and immerse myself in a dance of love
there is an encounter that gives us light
love between poet and crane

a song that brings secret words
flights, silences, eternal colors . . .

translated from the Spanish by Cristina Eisenberg

Espíritu De Grulla Y Espíritu Quechua

Para mirar la claridad
Que me ofrecen las aves
Llego a la orilla del río plateado
Me inclino y espero en silencio
Sobre el cielo azul la grulla me habla
con su vuelo y su canto
Entonces observo ojo de sol
Y espíritu de grulla que desciende del cielo
la luna observa tímidamente

desde la otra orilla del tiempo
la grulla llega y me dice:
soy tu canto, el grito de tu gente
la levedad del tiempo
en mi canto moran las voces de los muertos
es nuestro grito de lucha,
aqui está el dolor y la fuerza de lo incontenible
el paso del viento entre frías montañas
y la danza de amor a la creación
Mi espíritu quechua pregunta:

Dime espíritu de grulla,
Cuál es el enigma de tu danza en el cielo azul?
Dice espíritu de grulla:
cuando cuerpo muere
Crece espíritu de grulla, somos clan de estrella
Clan, de luna, clan de sol, clan de viento, clan de nube,
Clan de río, clan de maiz, clan de lluvia, clan de nieve,
Clan de tierra, clan árbol, clan buffalo, clan coyote, clan águila,
Clan ciervo, clan lobo, clan caballo, y así con todo elemento natural
Estrella en el cielo vuela, es espíritu de abuelos
luna en el cielo vuela, es el amor
Sol en el cielo vuela persigue la oscuridad
Nube en el cielo vuela, llama a colores del agua
Río en el cielo vuela para no morir en la tierra
Buffalo en el cielo vuela para vivir en su gente
Coyote y montaña en el cielo vuela para ahuyentar la pena,
Caballo en el cielo vuela para reconocer su pampa
Águila en el cielo vuela para preservar los sueños de la noche
Ciervo en el cielo vuela para espantar temores
Aguila en el cielo vuela para engendrar espíritu del viento
Entonces espíritu quechua habla de nuevo:
Ahora entiendo ave gris, mujer canto,
mensajera de los grandes espíritus de la tierra
eres poema escrito en el aire
canto de luz, grito del amanecer
danza guerrera del anochecer

desde ahora volare contigo
para guardar en precioso cofre
tu canto, el grito que alimenta el espíritu de esta tierra
amarilla.
Somos uno dice espíritu de grulla: tu canto y mi canto
Tu danza y mi danza en el infinito alumbrar de las estrellas.

Crane Spirit and Quechua Spirit

To see the clarity
That the birds offer me
I arrive at the shore of the silver river
I recline and listen in silence
Upon the blue sky the crane speaks to me
with her flight and song
Then I observe the eye of the sun
And the spirit of the crane that descends from the sky
the moon watches timidly

from the other shore of time
the crane arrives and tells me:
I am your song, the cry of your people
the lightness of time
in my song dwell the voices of the dead
it is our battle cry
here is the pain and the strength of that which can't be contained
the passage of the wind between cold mountains
the dance of love of creation
My Quechua spirit asks:
Tell me, crane spirit
What is the enigma of your dance in the blue sky?
The crane spirit says:
when the body dies
The crane spirit grows, we are of the clan of the star
Clan of the moon, clan of the sun, clan of the wind, clan of the clouds
Clan of the river, clan of the maiz, clan of the rain, clan of the snow
Clan of the earth, tree clan, buffalo clan coyote clan, eagle clan
Deer clan, wolf clan, horse clan and thus with all the natural elements
Star in the sky flies, it is the spirit of grandparents
Moon in the sky flies, it is love
Sun in the sky flies, chasing darkness
Cloud in the sky flies, calling the colors of the water

River in the sky flies so as to not die on earth
Buffalo in the sky flies to live with his people
Coyote and mountain in the sky fly to frighten away the pain
Horse in the sky flies to recognize his plain
Eagle in the sky flies to preserve the night's dreams
Deer in the sky flies to scare away fears
Eagle in the sky flies to bring forth the spirit of the wind
And then Quechua spirit will speak anew:
Now I understand gray bird, woman song,
messenger of the great spirits of the earth
you are a poem written in the air
a song of light, a cry of awakening
a warrior dance of dusk
from now on I will fly with you

to guard in a beautiful coffer
your song, the cry that nourishes the spirit of this
yellow earth.
We are one says the spirit of the crane: your song and my song
Your dance and my dance in the stars' infinite light.

translated from the Spanish by Cristina Eisenberg

Palabra De Abuelo

Palabra de abuelo—no sigas a ese pájaro gris—,
que es espíritu y lleva al despeñadero,
es pájaro de muerte.
Palabra de abuela—no juegues con fuego—,
que hace orinar en cama,
es frió dentro de cuerpo.
Palabra de Taita—haz caso al abuelo—,
hay que pagar para cazar.

Palabra de mamita—haz caso a la abuela—,
hay que pagar para jugar con el fuego.
Palabra de pájaro gris—abuelo de mal agüero—,
es hombre desconfiado.
Palabra de fuego—abuela de mal presagio—,
es mujer maliciosa.
Palabra de mi corazón—bienvenido el misterio—,
alienta este canto.

A Word From Grandfather

A word from grandfather—do not follow that grey bird
for it is a spirit and it takes you to the precipice,
it is a bird of death.
A word from grandmother—do not play with fire
for it makes you wet the bed,
it is cold within the body.
A word from taita—heed your grandfather,
you must pay to hunt.

A word from mama—heed your grandmother,
you must pay to play with fire.
A word from the grey bird—the grandfather of ill omen
is a distrustful man.
A word from the fire—the grandmother of ill omen
is an evil-minded woman.
A word from my heart—you are welcome mystery,
inspirit this song.

translated from the Spanish by Nicolás Suescún

Sueños

Dichosa la noche
dueña del sueño desnudo de la hierba de páramo
porque es libre en lo alto de la montaña.

Dichosa el agua
que hace crecer las flores de esta tierra amenazada
porque ante la muerte otorga la belleza.

Dichoso el abuelo
que tuvo tiempo de morir y cantar en medio de la guerra.

Dichosos los sueños de la gente de la tierra azul
porque son de tambor, de río, de pechos de mujer,
de terca raíz que esquiva la muerte . . .

Dreams

Happy the night
master of the naked dreams of the paramo
because it is free in the mountain tops.

Happy the water
that makes the flowers grow on this menaced earth
because it grants beauty facing death.

Happy the grandfather
who had time to die and to sing in the midst of war.

Happy the dreams of the people of the blue earth
because they are of drum, of river, of women's breasts,
of stubborn root that evades death . . .

   translated from the Spanish by Nicolás Suescún

Todo Está Dicho

No tengo nada que decir
sobre el tiempo y el espacio que se nos
vino encima.

Todo está dicho.

Que hablen los ríos desde su agonía,
que hablen las serpientes que se arrastran
por ciudades y pueblos,
que algo digan las palomas desde sus
ensangrentados nidos;
yo,
hijo de tierras ancestrales;
no tengo nada que decir.

Todo está dicho.

Esos soles transcurridos
también algo tendrán en su memoria,
aquellas lunas que lloran con la lluvia
algo tendrán en sus recuerdos de amargura,
los árboles, los peces,
el ultimo arco iris venerado
tendrán algo entre sus quejas;

yo,
hijo de dolores y esperanzas
nada tengo que decir
Todo está dicho.

Everything Has Been Said

I have nothing to say
about the time and the space that
have come upon us.

Everything has been said.

Let the rivers talk in their agony,
let the serpents that crawl
through cities and towns talk,
let the doves say something from their
nests spattered with blood;
I,
son of the ancestral lands,
have nothing to say.

Everything has been said.

Those suns that have passed by
must also have something in their memory,
those moons that cry with the rain
must also have something in their bitter memories,
the trees, the fish,
the last worshipped rainbow
must have something in their complaints;
I,
son of pains and of hopes
have nothing to say.

Everything has been said.

translated from the Spanish by Nicolás Suescún

Rosa Chávez

Ri oj abaj xkoj qetal ruka katanalaj ch'ich'

Ri oj ab'aj xkoj qetal ruk'a k'atanalaj ch'ich'
Xk'at ri qab'aq'wach
Xojilon ruk' ri tzolq'ominaq qawach
Q'eq taq jul
Kqab'iq' qib' ruk' pa ri najil
Ri kamikal kuyuq'uj qaj ri qak'axk'ol
Ri utz'i' kureq' ri qaqolotajik
Kuchub'aj ri k'otk'ob'naqalaj qak'u'x
Ri uk'ok'al ri ulew man junam ta chik
Ketzaq lo uwach taq che e ma'j k'u na
Xaq chi owal xoj k'iyik
Chi tz'uj chi tz'uj pa uk'u'x taq ri jul
Jeri' qapisik xub'an ri utz'ininem
Ri nimalaj majb'alil

Las piedras fuimos marcadas con hierro candente

Las piedras fuimos marcadas con hierro candente
quemados nuestros ojos
vimos con la mirada volteada
agujeros negros
tragándonos en la infinidad
la muerte chineaba nuestra desgracia
su perro lamia nuestras heridas
escupiendo
nuestra conciencia lacerada
ya el sabor de la tierra no era el mismo
los frutos caían antes de madurar
a escondidas fuimos creciendo
gota a gota en lo profundo de las cuevas
así fue como nos envolvió el silencio
del gran comienzo.

We, stones, were branded by hot iron

We, stones, were branded by hot iron
our eyes scorched
we saw through an inverted gaze
black holes
swallowing us in infinity
death cuddling our misfortune
his dog licking our wounds
spitting
our lacerated conscience
already the flavor of the earth was not the same
fruits fell before they ripened
we were growing clandestinely
drop by drop deep within the caves
it was in this way that the silence of the great beginning engulfed us

translated from Spanish by Gloria E. Chacón

Chaya'a b'e chwech rajawal ri b'e

Chaya'a b'e chwech rajawal ri b'e
Chaya'a b'e kinq'ax na
Kinb'in na apan chi upam ri
Ab'aja b'e
Ri xq'ajow ri amuxu'x
Pa we kaqiq'alaj b'e
Ri ktz'apin uchi' ri tz'ininem
Kinta toq'ob' che alaq xuquje'
laj taq tz'ikin ri kkixilij ri ko'alaj ch'ich'
kinq'ax na laj taq ab'aj
kinq'ax na laj taq che'
kinq'ax na laj taq awaj ri kkikoch' ri sutz'.
Xa kinq'ax na nub'e
Chaya'a b'e chi we ch'u'jarik ri kurech' ri nuwach
Kel lo chwe pa taq ki' taq tzij,
Ch'uch'uj taq tzij, e xojowsam, e paq'inaq,

Chya' alaq nub'e
Mat b'a chja'r ri nuch'uq'ab'
Chya'a la b'e chwe kinq'axej ri siwan, ri jomojik,
Chaya'a la b'e chwe kintzalij chi uwach wachoch
Mojo'q che b'ixan ri ixkanulab'
Mojo'q chi ri kitzijonik ri taq juyub' chechub'an ulo pa ri qachi'.

Dame permiso espíritu del camino

Dame permiso espíritu del camino
regalame permiso
para caminar
por este sendero de cemento
que abrieron en tú ombligo
por esta autopista de viento
que corta el silencio
permiso también a ustedes
pájaros que rompen el tímpano del acero
permiso piedras
permiso plantas
permiso animales que resisten en la neblina.
Dejame pasar camino
deja que esta rabia que desorbita mis ojos
se me salga en palabras dulces,
palabras finas, zarandeadas, reventadas,
dejame pasar
que mi voluntad no se pierda
dejame cruzar el barranco, la hondonada,
dejame por favor regresar a mi casa
antes de que los volcanes canten
antes de que el discurso de los cerros
escupa en nuestras bocas.

Spirit of this path grant me permission

Spirit of this path grant me permission
grant me permission
to walk
on this road of cement
that was opened in your bellybutton
on this freeway of wind
that cuts silence
permission also to you
birds that break the eardrum of steel
Permission stones
permission plants
permission animals that resist in the haze.
Allow me to pass your way
Let the anger that crazes my eyes
Depart in sweet words,
fine, shaken, ruptured words,
allow me to pass through
that my will does not get lost
allow me to cross the ravine,
to cross the precipice, the dale,
please allow me to return home
before the volcanoes sing
before the discourse of the hills spits in our mouths.

El espíritu se va si no lo cuidamos

El espíritu se va si no lo cuidamos
agarra su propio camino si se incomoda
toma su propia medicina si se enferma
se aleja
como si nada sobre el mar
no dice adiós
se va sin remordimientos,
sin culpas,
en su ausencia
dejamos de ser sagrados
nos volvemos algo sin nombre.

The spirit leaves us if we do not care for it

The spirit leaves us if we do not care for it
it finds its own path if it is discomfited
it makes its own medicine if it falls ill
it takes itself
without a qualm over the sea
it does bid goodbye
it goes without recriminations,
without blame,
in its absence
we should be sacred
we become something without a name.

translated from Spanish by Laura Ortega

Hace Un Mes

Hace un mes
ne a la capital
mi tata nos abandonó
y en la casa el hambre dolía,
yo trabajo en una casa

(la señora dice que de doméstica)
aunque no entiendo muy bien que es eso,
me dieron un disfraz de tela,
ese día lloré mucho, llore mucho
me daba vergüenza ponerlo
y enseñar las piernas,
la señora dice que en mi pueblo
todos somos shucos
por eso me baño todos los días
mi pelo largo lo cortaron
dice que por los piojos,
no puedo hablar bien castilla
y la gente se ríe de mí
mi corazón
se pone triste,
ayer fui a ver a mi prima
voy contenta porque puse mi corte,
el chofer no quería parar
y cuando iba a bajar, rápido arrancó,
—apurate india burra—me dijo
yo me caí y me raspé la rodilla
risa y risa estaba la gente
mi corazón se puso triste
dice mi prima
que ya me voy a acostumbrar
que el domingo vamos al parque central
que hay salones para bailar
con los grupos que llegan a la feria de allá,
de mi pueblo,
estoy en mi cuartito
contando el dinero que me pagaron
menos el jabón y dos vasos que quebré
la señora dice que soy bien bruta

no entiendo porque me tratan mal
¿acaso no soy gente pues?

Hace Un Mes

A month ago
I came to the capital
our grandfather abandoned us
and at home hunger was hurting us
I worked in a house
(the lady of the house said I was a domestic)
although I do not know what that means.
They gave me a fancy cloth dress,
that day I cried so much, I cried so much
I was ashamed to wear it
and let others see my legs,
the lady of the house says that in my town
we are filthy
that is why I take a bath every day
they cut my long hair
she says because of the lice
I can't speak the right way
and people laugh at me
my heart becomes sad,
yesterday I went to visit my cousin who's a woman
I go happy because I put on my nice dress,
the driver did not want to stop
and when I wanted to get down, he took off fast,
"Hurry up, you stupid Indian," he told me
I fell and scraped my knee
people were laughing so hard
my heart grew sad
my cousin says
I will get used to it
that we'll go to the park in the middle of town on Sunday
that there are rooms where we can dance
with the people that come from the fair over there,
from my town,

I'm in my little room,
counting the money they've given me
not counting the money for the soap and the two glasses I broke
the lady of the house says I'm dumb

I don't know why they treat me badly
I'm a person, aren't I?

translated from Spanish by Laura Ortega

Los ojos de los desaparecidos hacia adentro

Los ojos de los desaparecidos miran hacia adentro
no se pueden cerrar amarrados en el tiempo
flotan sus nombres al viento como bandera de nadie
dicen adiós esperando el retorno.

The eyes of the vanished look inward

The eyes of the vanished look inward
they cannot be closed tied to time
their names fly in the wind like a flag belonging to no one
they say goodbye waiting to return.

translated from Spanish by Laura Ortega

Norys Odalia Saavedra Sanchez

Me lacero

from *Del libro: De Áridas Soledades,* 2007

Me lacero
la piel

Hay un dios
que ya no anda
no es

Se escondió
en mi cuerpo

No
lo veo

I lacerate

I lacerate
my skin

There is a god
that no longer moves
it is non-existent

It has hidden itself
in my body

I do not
see it

translated from Spanish by Laura Ortega

Hoja que trae lluvia

from *Del libro: De Áridas Soledades,* 2007

Hoja que trae lluvia
Me descalzo
y piso brisa

Siempre descalza camino
a vieja manera
de indios

No importa lo que clava
en los pies
No importa pisar el barro

Desentiéndete
Dice el río:
¡Andando! Hoja que trae lluvia

Y arrodillo
mis animales
conmigo

Leaf that brings the rain

Leaf that brings the rain
I go barefoot
and encounter the breeze

Always barefoot I walk
in the old way
of the Indians

It is not important
what is fixed onto the feet
It is not important to touch baked clay

Feign ignorance
The river says:
Moving! Leaf of the rain

I kneel down
my animals
with me

translated from Spanish by Laura Ortega

Si el salitre de mar

from *Naranjos largos de viento*

Si el salitre de mar
viene a buscarme

Encontrará extendidas
trenzas indígenas
        en mi cabello

Ocupará el terreno mustio de las casas

La carreta de las cabras
en la memoria de los cueros

Alumbraría en mí como una vela

If the salt of the sea

If the salt of the sea
comes to seek me

It will discover
the unbraided lengths
        of my hair

It will inhabit the gloomy insides of the houses

The wagon of the nanny goats
of the memories of the hides

It will glow in me like a candle

> translated from Spanish by Laura Ortega

Secadal

> from *Caza de Animales en Flor,* 2009

> a mi prima Indira, por la lucha de la tierra

Hay un retiro de laderas
volteadas abajo

El veneno da golpes al día
deja su canto a los buitres

El escalofrió de hormigas huye

Mil insectos dejan sus cuerpos
cielitos de candela
ramales negros

Una cigarra dice:
Sólo se vive un verano

Secadal

For my cousin Indira, for the fight over the land

There is a retreat of mountainsides
which are turned upside-down

Poison deals blows during the day
it leaves its song to the vultures

The shiverings caused by ants disappear

A thousand insects leave their bodies
little heavens of light
black branches

A grasshopper says:
A life is only a summer's length

> *Secadal*: dry, barren ground
>
> translated from Spanish by Laura Ortega

Odilón Ramos Boza

Llama

Yana llamachay
hatun urqu hina,
chaska ñawicha
tusukachanki
yana puyukunapi
hawachampi.

Yana llamachay
lastaramuptinqa
qatun urqukunapa
ñawichan hina
kapuwanki.

Llama

Mi negra llamita
eres como los cerros grandes,
ojos de lucero,
bailas
sobre las nubes oscuras.

Mi negra llamita.
Cuando cae la nieve
Son como de los cerros inmensos
tus grande ojos negros.
Mi llamita.

A Poem to My Llama

My little black llama
You are just like a big mountain,
your eyes like a candle light
You dance
on top of dark clouds

My little black llama,
when the snow falls
your big black eyes
are like giant mountains
My little llama.

translated from *haylli and poesía* by Marleen Haboud

Sobre los Campos

(Through the Fields)

Leonel Lienlaf

Bajan Gritando Ellos Sobre los Campos

Wirarünmu nagpay yengün
Iweñünmu küpaley yen gün
Pepan ñi pu che
Umül-umülü-yengün
Wente Mapu
Wentemew rupay pu winka
Allfüli ti mapu yengün
Allfüli ñi piuke

Konün ina ñi rukamew
Ka ngüman
Eimi may allkütumekeimi
Allkütumuchi ka puen pipingen

Rupa-rupangey tripantu
Rupa-rupangey mapu
Kenchalen ka deuma
Pepi dünguwelan

Allkütumuchi ka puen
Pipingen.

Bajan Gritando Ellos Sobre los Campos

Bajan gritando
ellos sobre los campos
silbando por los esteros
corro a ver a mi gente,
a mi sangre
pero ya están tendidos
sobre el suelo
sobre ellos pasan los winkas/huincas
hiriendo de muerte la tierra,
dividiendo mi corazón

Entré en busca de mi calor
a mi casa ardiendo
Brotó el estero de mis lágrimas lloviendo sobre mis pies

¿Ustedes entienden mis lágrimas?
Escuchen al aire explicarlas

Están pasando los años,
están pasando los nidos
sobre el fuego,
está pasando la tierra
y ya me estoy perdiendo
entre las palabras

Escuchen hablar a mis lágrimas

They Come Down Yelling Through the Fields

They come down yelling
through the fields
whistling through the marshes
I run to see my people
my blood
but they are already lying
on the floor
over them the white men walk
fatally wounding the land
splitting up my heart

I came in looking for my warmth
in my burning home
the marsh of my raining tears sprung
on my feet

Do you all understand my tears?
listen to the air explain them

Years are going by
nests are going by
on the fire
the earth is going by
and I am getting lost
in words

Listen to my tears speak

translated from Mapuche and Spanish by Irene Beibe

Palabras Dichas

Kaley mi pin
kochkÜlla dunguenew,
mapu dunguenew.
Epe ngümafun.
Chukao dunguenew
mi külleñu
müley mi eluafiel
rayen.

Palabras Dichas

"Es otra tu palabra"
me habló el copihue,
me habló la tierra.
Casi lloré.
"Tus lágrimas debes
dársela a las flores"
me habló el pájaro chucao.

Palabras Dichas

"Another one is your word"
said the copihue to me
said the earth to me.
I almost cried.
"Your tears you should
give to the flowers"
the chucao bird said to me.

> *Copihue*: National flower of Chile
> *Chucao*: A bird similar to the thrush

> translated from Mapuche and Spanish by Irene Beibe

Lluvia

Nagpay tapül rayen kechi
kiñeke wag nagpay
umülünmu rupay
kachill ñi piuke
ka füchküllmaenew ñi mollfüñ.

Lluvia

Bajó como pétalos de flores
gota a gota
y cayó sobre mi cabeza
luego se escurrió
cerca de mi corazón
refrescando mis venas sedientas.

Lluvia

It fell like flower petals
drop by drop
and landed on my head
and then it slipped
close to my heart
refreshing my thirsty veins

translated from Mapuche and Spanish by Irene Beibe

Morela Del Valle Maneiro Poyo

En mi Puerto

En mi puerto contemplando el río
Pasó el gavilán
Pasó la garza
Pasó el paují.

Pasó la ola ondulando su mirada
y en un minuto de siglos . . .
fue narrándome cruzando el río,
como los pueblos se han liberado.

PUORO'TOPOOPO

Puoro'topopo tunna eneerü'dako
Neepato apaaka'no
Neepato awuürü
Neepato wooko.

Neepaatoi shuru'kuru botampiopo'türü düünedan
koi'ñopokonoro penaatonon beepa'kasankon pooko düru'puaman . . .
tunnapatorü'dako tunnata,
otuwaara po'purü'kon ata'ñakaññe na'miatu.

At My River Port

While at my river port, I contemplate
through here passed the hawk
through here passed the heron
through here passed the *paují*.

A wave came, its gaze undulating,
a minute of centuries,
and it told me, as it crossed the river,
of the people's freedom.

translated from Spanish and Kari'ña by Laura Ortega

Navegando

Llovizna sobre mi canoa el canto de mis abuelos
Caribes (Pía, Makunaima, Marawaka).
gotea en recuerdos mi origen ...
Desde el vientre hibrido de mí madre–anaconda–primordial
¡Sigo mi travesía!

Reaparece el mito
de mi hermano Orión
brota de la conciencia de
nuestro pueblo.

¡Una tormenta me despertó!
para no olvidar la creación.

TUNNATA TOOPOTOTO

Kono'poshichi kuri'yara re'taka kono'pasan tanko barerü'kon
Kari'ñakon (Pía, Makunaima, Marawaka).
puanarü´taka wonumuenkarü´mua wü'pakato'pompo biñño ...
Amu poosetü biñño aau suaano–akoduumuo–i'punooro
¡wü'sannoro tunnata!

Nepa'kairopa takaari'shan
düaakono Piee´tümü
nepa'kai marakanoja
tau'rotopo biññoro.

¡O'bin apooto konoopo moorü du´pakai!
ta'karü'puona penaarono epa'kasankon.

The Voyage

It is as if the song of my Carib
(*Pía, Makunaima, Marawaka*) ancestors
is rain falling softly on my canoe
as if the drops are reminders of my origin . . .
From the hybrid womb of my primeval anaconda mother,
I continue my voyage!

The myth of
my kinsman Orion
is never far from the conscience of
our people.

A storm wakens me!
So that I may never forget creation.

> translated from Spanish and Kari'ña by Laura Ortega

ABAANA'IMIE

(PAJARO CANTOR QUIEN INVOCA A WANAWANARI QUIEN A SU VEZ
ANUNCIA EN LA MADRUGADA LA VENIDA DEL AGUILA Y
SE LLEVARA EN SUS ALAS EL ESPIRITU DESENCARNADO O ALMA
DIFUNTA AL MAXIMO CIELO).

ABAANA'IMIE

Abuela Abanaa'imie, cantora y danzante
¿Cuántas lenguas hablan en el cielo?
¿Cuando darás la vuelta al sol?

Abuela Abaana'imie, me lanzaste de tu placenta,
silbando mi voz amaneciendo.
Solo la hoja sabe el canto de quienes somos.

Abuela Abaana'imie cruzaste doce cielos
¿Dime, sabes mi destino?
Luciérnaga, susurras versos al oído de la luna.
siembra mi corazón en tus cenizas.

Abuela Abaana'imie ¿A quién contaré mis desvelos?
recuerdas al hombre ojos azabaches,
y las hormigas en mi ombligo
donde abrasé y besé la oscuridad del placer.

Abuela Abaana'imie, soy madre de gemelos,
los espíritus están en el fogón de mi vientre,
ordénales a salir junto a tus hermanos pájaros
en el amanecer.

Abuela Abaana'imie, pasaste la culebra de agua,
lloraste sobre la creación alfarera de tu vida
moldeada en tus manos.

Abuela Abaana'imie, descarnada, sin máscaras
llevas las tonadas de los cinco mundos en tu maraca
la tierra te reclama, recogeré tus pasos.

ABAANA'IMIE

Nootü abaana' imie baare eemü, waatoto
¿O'toro auranaanokon ka'satu kaaputa?
¿Ootü daako veedu ü'müntümü awü'torü?

Nootü abaana'imie memaapoi o'movi'pio viñño
Emaamü'ta dau'bran otaaki'ñata,
Tü'naka aarü shipiiyu baarerü pusan.
Süano, notü anookanmue kataatu.

Nootü abaana'imie ooko aññatone ere'taka ookokaapu mipiaatopo'tü
¿Ka'cho muupusa ooto wairü?
Tüpürü'na otajpa'ko nunno pianarü'taka merupuae
Müarakana'jo aru'kako ade'mu'jo re'ta.

Nootü abaana'imie ¿anookü'wa ekari'chürü'wa , wüotuwükatoopo
Beenkokon'yo puo'betü'puo.
Eba'rumü'puo eba'matoopopo apo'chopoopoyo.

Nootü abaana'imie, aseepirü'dan saano meeba
A'karükon puo'setü atuunu taama
Pia'kamo'topoko, adasakarükonwa toonorokon'wa,
Emaamüruta.

Nootü abaana'imie akoodumu mipiaatoi
Mataamoi ani'chürü'puo adaakarü re'ta.
ada'ñarü'ta shürü'puo.

Nootü abaana'imie, ada'karü ere'napoturü atu'nemü'ja
Marooda amara'karüta aññatone paaporo noono ponokon etükon
Noono adaaki'miano adeemarü awü'tapo'topo samo'isha.

ABAANA'IMIE

ABAANA'IMIE: SINGING BIRD WHICH REMINDS ONE OF THE
WANAWANARI [SEAGULL] WHICH HERALDS THE ARRIVAL OF
DAWN AND THE APPROACH OF THE EAGLE

AND WHICH BEARS ON ITS WINGS A FLESHLESS SPIRIT OR SOUL
TO THE HIGHEST POINT IN THE SKY.

ABAANA'IMIE

Grandmother *Abaana'imie,* singer and dancer
How many languages are spoken in the sky?
How long is your journey around the sun?

Grandmother *Abaana'imie,* you tore me from your placenta,
my new-born voice hissing.
Only the leaf knows who we truly are.

Grandmother *Abaana'imie,* you flew across twelve skies

Tell me, do you know my fate?
Glow-worm, you whisper into the moon's ear.
Give light to my heart with your death.

Grandmother *Abaana'imie,* Who will I tell of my white nights?
You remember the man with the darkest eyes
and the butterflies in my stomach
where I kissed and embraced pleasant darkness.

Grandmother *Abaana'imie*, I am the mother of twins,
whose spirits are in the hearth of my womb,
to be born simultaneously with your brother birds at dawn.

Grandmother Abaana'imie, you passed the snake of water,
wept over the potter's view of your life
which was made by your hands.

Grandmother Abaana'imie, fleshless, unmasked
you have the songs of the five worlds in your *maraca*
the world calls for you, I clear your path.

    translated from Spanish and Kari'ña by Laura Ortega

ARCO IRIS

Miro, a través de mis ojos;
el ADN, la llave de la vida.

Miro, el axis del mundo,
la escalera celestial,
los espíritus dobles,
la potencia vital,
la mecha de lino trenzado.

Miro, las nervaduras de las hojas,
que codifican el origen del mundo,
y se convierten en un panel solar.

Miro, las plantas: los helechos,
las ixoras, las orquídeas
y todas las flores: rojas, violetas, amarillas
azules, blancas, naranjadas y rosadas.

Aromatizadas y perfumadas en el espacio sideral
las flores se van alineándose ordenadamente
en un arco iris universal.

PARAAMU

Seneeda dümuuru'ke;
mooro ADN, amaamü mü'topo.

Seneeda, amanto'po vojkürürü,
kaapu chi'sharerarü,
akarü'kon okonokon,
pori'ñome cha'vonooro mojkoma,
kunuurimia esuuru kapü'puo.

Seneeda aarü meerükon,
kamanto'ko, veepa'karü viñño
veedu aveenü kanookasa.

Seneeda, i'chutanokon emüjdatone:
bebe raarü pookonoko, tapürü'piiramo:
ye'pioro tapürükamokon, taapiran, to'kiññan, tü'kiiran,
azules, taamunan, tuku'ruran, tusuuviran.

Ama'ntopo po'nodan, tüpuoposhiñeke.
asevaaro epürürü'kon künüsatu ü'puoto'me
paraamu'wa pa'poro viontotojme.

Rainbow

I see, in front of my eyes,
the ADN, the key to the world.

I see, the world turning,
the heavenly staircase,
the twin spirits,
the essential potential,
the braided linen wick.

I see the veins of the leaf,
which signal the beginning of the world's creation,
and they transform into a solar shield.

I see, the plants, the ferns,
the *ixoras,* the orchids,
and all of the other flowers: red, purple, yellow,
blue, white, orange and pink.

Scented and fragrant in star-space
the flowers are aligning themselves perfectly
in a celestial rainbow.

translated from Spanish and Kari'ña by Laura Ortega

Juanita Pahdopony

Taa Nꚉmꚉ Tekwa Hꚉrꚉunꚉ

Sobesꚉ tsa tekwaiehtꚉ
una nu tek waipu
subeh Nꚉmꚉnꚉ mai aie
unꚉ tek wai yu
penah kama wai kꚉ nania

Ꚉkitsi tse se hꚉitsi tah ka
Nꚉmꚉ Tekwai?yu
Ta Nꚉmꚉ Tekwapꚉha tsa tu yi mia yaa
Subetꚉ mah.

The Loss of Our Language

A long time ago
when animals
could talk,
the language
of *the people*
was spoken,
sweet—like sugar.

Today, few speak
Comanche
its loss—a bitter lesson.
That is all.

translated from Comanche by the author

Lindantonella Solano

TALE>EWAIN-AMIGO

Encuentro y diálogo entre un wayuu y un español.
Pütchi nanje wanne wayuu otta wanne arijuna.
te llamas?
Anshi pa talewain,
Kasachii pünulia arijuna?
te llamas?
Vale no os entiendo?
Nnojotsu totüjaiinau tüu punuiikakat talalaula, ware ashajaa anash ta ya.
El alijuna no entiende, se va
Vale no te, sos un ignorante . . .
Una lanza de palabras
500 años sigue abriendo brechas entre los hispanoamericanos.
"Mulekat nnojolü in wat'ajain watujanin a'u wanne
putchi sünainje wane ashajaa anash su lu>utüü
wounmaimpa miou hispanoamericanos.

Tale>Ewain-Amigo

Encounter and dialogue between a native Wayuu and a Spaniard
Püchi nanje waane wayuu otta wanne arijuna.
What's your name?
Anshipa talewain.
Kasachii pünulia arijuna?
What's your name? Come on, I don't understand you.
Nnojotsu totüjaiinau tüu punuiikakat talalaula, ware ashajaa anash ta ya.
The Wayuu is not understood; he leaves.
Come on, don't be stupid.
A barrage of words
500 years of widening the rift between Spanish-speakers
Mulekat nnojolü in wat'ajain watujanin a'u wanne
putchi sünainje wane ashajaa anash su lu>utüü
wounmaimpa miou Spanish-speakers.

translated from Spanish by Laura Ortega

El Isho Cautivo

a todos los secuestrados

El isho
Lo tienen cautivo
su trino ausente
ante los días
descubiertos,
el corazón de trupillos y dividivis
extraña su compañía
el rumbo de las horas
es controlada por el desespero . . .

Soltaran aquel cantor?
alas de libertad caminan
piden respuesta . . .
cuando será su regreso?
Hoy preso
entre la jungla de

rapaces aves
lejanas o cercanas . . .
indescifrable
los jayechiis . . .
Ante el rumiar de los espejos
el canto del cardenal
pronuncia un alud de silencio
en esa virgen
mañana,
el ocaso te despidió . . .
La tierra espera
pronto escuchar tu
cálido trinar . . .

The Captive Isho
All the hostages

The isho
We have captive
trino his absent
days before the
discovered
the heart of trupillos and dividivis
strange company
the course of hours
is controlled by the desperation . . .

Release that singer?
wings of freedom walk
ask answer . . .
when is your return?
Today prisoner
the jungle

Birds of prey
distant or close . . .
indecipherable
the jayechiis . . .
Before the cud of mirrors
Cardinal singing
pronounces an avalanche of silence
in the virgin
morning,
You sacked the sunset . . .

The expected land
soon hear your
warm doctrine . . .

Dreams of Sekurru

Kashi savor the flavor
wind,
when the water in the dance
eyes of the walker,
children Mareiwa
spectra are kai . . .

A weeping blood
and thorns spring from mma
yorujaa travels . . .

Even still
juyaa exile,
still stuck
Be the Wayuu . . .

Los Sueños de Sekurru

Kashi saborea el aroma
del viento,
cuando danza el agua en los
ojos del caminante,
los hijos de Mareiwa
son espectros de kai . . .

Un llanto con sangre
y espinas brotan de mma
recorre yorujaa . . .

Aun sigue en
destierro juyaa,
clavada sigue
Sed de los Wayuu . . .

Queen of Shadows

a Alejandra Pizarnik

The queen of shadows
bleeding broken words
sweats crimes
flowing Mirror
delirious and modesty,
reflects a trunk
copulate with death,
birds and purple
in the cage of destiny
in full sun.

Reina De Sombras

a Alejandra Pizarnik

La reina de sombras
sangra palabras rotas
suda delitos
que fluyen del espejo
delirante y pudoroso,
refleja un tronco
copulando con la muerte,
y pájaros púrpuras
en la jaula del destino
en pleno ocaso.

Paula Nelson

A-ni-no-gi-i De-s-gv-i

A-ni-no-gi-i De-s-gv-i
Wa-na-i A-ni-ne-ga
A-ni-wo-ni De-s-gv-i
Ha-tv-gi-sdi-sge-sdi Wa-na-i A-ni-wo-ni-s-gv-i
Ga-no-lv-v-sga U-no-le
Hi-go-ti Di-ya-sv
De-s-gv A-na-da-so-la-de-sgi
A-ni-no-gi-s-gv Ha-tv-gi-di-ge-sdi
Ha-tv-gi-sdi-sge-sdi Wa-na-i A-ni-wo-ni-s-gv-i

Trees Are Singing

Trees are singing
Soft they Speak
Speaking are the trees
Hear them softly speaking
Blowing is the wind
you see it coming
The trees are waving,
Singing, Listen to them
Hear them softly speaking

translated from Cherokee by the author

Land Song

(from the hearts of the elders)

ge-s-di hi e-lo dv-ga-ni-gi-s-sv
ge-s-di hv-la-hi-yu di-ge-si
a-gwa-da-nv-do hi-a ga-da
hi-a a-mo a-gwa-da-nv-to

I-ya hi-a e-lo
a-gwa-du-li i-hi tsi-go-tv-di
na-s-gi a-yv-wi ge-hv a-ya
a-le s-gwu a-ya i-yu-s-di i-hi

Land Song

(from the hearts of the elders)

I will not leave this land
I will never go
The dirt is my heart
The water is my soul

I am this land
I want you to see
That I am human
And you are just like me

translated from Cherokee by the author

Hilario Chacin

Sekurulu (Sokurulu)

Osho'lujashi waneepia
Sekuruutkai,
Süka nüpolüin aja'atüsü mojuui nutuma
Sa'anasiakaa wajiirü.
Nüshottüin yosu mülaa'tkalü atüünoutta,
Nüshottüin aipia anakalü a'wala,
Nüshottüin alia jemetakalü sheejuu
Ajapü,
Nüshottüin ata jiruuttakalü ato'uta,
Nüshottüin ichii josokalü asa'uta,
Nüshottüin mapua wüitakalü ashe'ein,
Nüshottüin paliruwain jintüi kayüürai,
Nüshottüin patsua kasa'aulekaa jümaa laütaain.
Aaschijaashi Kute'ena saalí süpüshua'aya
Atkünüshi sekurulu süka jatü.
Achiyajaashi maluwa
Eeimalaa müsi'a tü atkawaakaa.

Pájaro carpintero

Corta que corta
El pájaro carpintero,
Su hacha cruel acecha la flora
De mi hermosa guajira.
Corta el cardón de brazos morenos,
Corta el Cuji de hermosas cabelleras,
Corta la caraña de manos perfumadas,
Corta el palo Brasil de piel arrugada,
Corta el dividivi de piernas resecas,

Corta el yabo de vestido verde,
Corta el caimito el niño malcriado,
Corta la peonía, la piernona y obesa.
Y en defensa de todos sale el
Indio desnudo disparando al pájaro
Carpintero con su flecha.
Lo intermedió palo santo
Y se calmó la contienda.

Woodpecker

Cut by cut
The woodpecker
Cuts the flowers off my beautiful *guajira* with its cruel hatchet.
It cuts the cardon cactus with its brown arms,
It cuts the cuji tree of the lovely ladies,
It cuts the fan-leaved palm tree of perfumed hands,
It cuts the Brazil wood tree with the wrinkled skin,
It cuts the dividivi tree with the dry legs,
It cuts the *yabo* in its green dress,
It cuts the star apple the bad-mannered child
It cuts the peony, those with heavy legs and those who are obese.
And to defend all of these
the Indian emerges naked
to shoot at the wood-pecking
bird with his arrow.
The holy wood interrupted the bird
and its attack was stopped.

translated from Wayuu and Spanish by Laura Ortega

Aka'lakui (aka'lapüi)

¡A'waatchii aka'lakuikana!
¡Awaataashii aka'lakuikana!
¡Ayonnajüshii aka'lakuikana!
¡Asirajüshii aka'lakuikana!

¡Olojushii aka'lakuikana!
¡Eküshii mapa aka'lakuikana!
¡A'wanajaashii sünain wawain aka'lakuikana!
¡Aijiraashii aka'lakuikana!

¡Ako'ojiraashii aka'lakuikana!
¡A'yalajüshii aka'lakuikana!
¡Ousajiraashii aka'lakuikana!
¡Shaaitüshii aka'lakuikana!

Los Duendes

¡Los duendes gritan!
¡Los duendes corren!
¡Los duendes saltan!
¡Los duendes ríen!

¡Los duendes cazan!
¡Los duendes comen miel!
¡Los duendes se convierten
En vientos huracanados!
¡Los duendes aman!

¡Los duendes se abrazan!
¡Los duendes lloran!
¡Los duendes se besan!
¡Los duendes juegan!

The Imps

The imps scream!
The imps run!
The imps jump!
The imps laugh!

The imps hunt!
The imps eat honey!
The imps transform themselves
into hurricane-force winds!
The imps love!

The imps embrace each other!
The imps cry!
The imps kiss each other!
The imps play!

> translated from Wayuu and Spanish by Laura Ortega

Nümajala yosu

Tamüsü tü jo'uttaikalü:
Pu'unapa püküjapa tanüiki
Namüin tepichikana namaa jima'aliikana,
Sulu'u mma aluwataanakalü alu'u
Natuma waneejena.

Nnojolinnapa emi'ijüin yoshushula,
Nnojoliinnapa nekeein tachon,
Nnojolinnapa ashijaweein na'wala süka yoshushula.

Talatapü'üsü laakaa
Shi'rüin waima tepichi emi'jüin shiroku
¿Jamüshiiche maa'in nayüülajaka taya?

El manifiesto del cardón

Le dije a la brisa:
Id y llevadle mi mensaje
A los niños y jóvenes
De esta tierra irredenta.

Han dejado de jugar con mis brazos,
Han dejado de comer mis frutos,
Han dejado de lavar sus cabellos con mi corazón.

Antes se alegraba la casimba.
Ver miles de niños jugueteando en ella.
No entiendo, ¿por qué me abandonan?

The Speech of the Cardon Cactus

I said to the breeze:
Go and deliver my message
To the children and youth
Of this land that is not truly theirs.

They no longer play with my arms,
They no longer eat my fruit,
They no longer wash their hair with my heart.

The cacimba used to be filled with joy,
Seeing the multitudes of children playing on her.
I don't understand. Why do they leave me?

translated from Wayuu and Spanish by Laura Ortega

Ariruma Kowii

Vivitaman

May sumak sumak kausailla
tukui pacha, tukui kausai kanki
rikuipi sumak muskui shina
shamunki

May sumak sumak kausailla
Kanpak rimaika
juyaiwan, rimaykunata
juyuna rimanakuikunapi
tikrachishpa
sinchi kausaikunata
alli kausaiman tikrachinki.

May sumak sumak kausailla
kushikuita rikuimanta
ñuka kausai, samai kausai
kausanata ushakunmi
tukui pachata, samaipi samanata
ushachun ushankimi.

May sumak sumak kausailla
kanpak kausay wayrashna kuyurinmi
ñukanchipak muskuita, tarinakunata
kaita chaita apashpa, kishpirik mannaman
apanata ushankimi.

May sumak sumak kausailla
jatun rimanakuishina Kanpak makika
yanaparina pachata kausachiwanmi
man riksishka kausayta juyachiwanmi
kanpak kausaipi, sumac sumakta
punchayachiwanmi.

A, *Virginia*

La vida
La vida eres Tú
Tu Mirada caudalosa
Inundandome de vertientes
Que nacen
En cada parpadeo tuyo.

Tus palabras
Eclipsadas de ternura
Transformando cada silaba
En conciertos de amor
En tratados indispensables
Para dshilar, las complejidades
De la vida.

Tu sonrisa
Apoyada en mi pecho
Acarreando hacia mi pulso
La serenidad, el equilibrio
De las constelaciones.
Tus inquietudes
Flotando en mi regazo
Navegando en canoas y caballitos
De totora
Van transportando
Nuestros retors y nuestros sueños
A la orilla, que aun nos llama
Y nos espera.

Tus manos
Envolviendome en su discurso
llevandome a compartir
la solidaridad de todos los horizontes
el amor valcaánico de tus entrañas
tu ser, tu vida
que son
mi vi da.

Life

Life
life is you
your plentiful look
flooding me with springs
born
each time your eyes blink.

Your words
eclipsed with tenderness
transforming each and every syllable
in concerts of love
in essential treaties
to unravel
life's complexities.

Your smile
resting on my breast
drawing to my pulse
the serenity, the balance
of the constellations.

Your concerns
floating on my lap
navigating on canoes and cattail
horses
transporting
our challenges, our dreams
to the shore that still calls us
and waits for us.

Your hands
wrapping me in their gesture
making me share
the solidarity of all horizons
the volcanic love of your entrails
your being, your life
which are my life.

> translated from Quechua (Kitchua) and
> Spanish by Marisa Estelrich

Shamukpacha Wañukrinmi

Sacha Mamaka punchan punchan jatarishp
tukuiwan sumak sumakta rimak karka
kunanaka, muskuikuna tukurinkapak kallarin
paipak rimay, chushak rimay tukushpa
wañunkapak kallarinmi.

Pishkukunapak takika
manchanay takikunashna uyarin
maytapash takishpa, chinkarinkapak kallarin
¿maipishi uyankapak rita ushashun?

Wayrak
wakcha tukushka, shaikushka
kipayashpa kipayashpa chayanmi.

Mayukunaka
mancharishka, wañukukshnallak
llaki llakita rikunakunmi

Pacha Mamata
yapata tukuchikuimanta
paipak shunkupi, imatapash churashpa
kausaimanta
jarkarinkapak kallarin
ashnaykunata shitankapak kallarinmi.

Yurakunaka
nana kaynashna
may sumac yurakunata pukuchinchu.

Shamuk pachaka
Wañunayta irkiyashkamanta
tulluyashka ñawita charikmanta
mana wacharishpallatak
wawata shitakrikukshina rikurinmi.

Kayaka
Wañukrikukshina rikurinmi
Kayaka, nana chayakrikukshnallak
rikurinchi.
Kaya, chayamunata ushachun
payta rikushpa katinkapak
alli yuyaita chaskichishunchik
kayata rikushpa katinkapak
pachamamapak unkuita, alli allita
wakaychishunchik.
Kayapak wawa sinchi sinchi kachun
wawata alli allita, chaskishunchik
shina paitaka, ninanta ukllashpa
ninanta kushikushpa
chaskichishunchik
shina paytaka
runa shutiwan
shuntichishunchik.

El Mañana Esta en Peligro

Los bosques, están perdiendo su vitalidad
sus diálogos agaonizan, pierden lucidez
comienzan, a enmudecer
sus sueños, se desmoronan
el silencio, empieza a reinar.

El canto
el canto de los pájaros
es leve y destemplado, sushimnos
¿en dónde podremos escuchar?

El aire llega, araposo, agotado
y con retraso

Los ríos, nos miran con amargura
y desesperación

Las entrañas de la tierra, se están
                    intoxicando
un mal aliento, empieza a expirer

Las plantas
ya no brotan con fuerza
con el mismo entusiasmo, de ayer

El mañana, temeroso
con el rostro pálido y su cuerpo
desnutrido
corre el riesgo de abortar

El mañana
el mañana, está en peligro
el mañana
corre el riesgo, de no llegar ¡mas!

El mañana, depende de nosotros
¡por eso! es fundamental
recuperar, nuestra razón de ser
es indispensable
cuidar bien su embarazo
hacer que su alumbramiento
sea un parto normal
que su hijo venga sana y
        vigoroso
y todas
todos podamos arrullarle
en nuestros brazos
todos podamos bautizarle
con el nombre
de:
¡Humanidad!

Tomorrow Is in Danger

The woods are losing their vitality
its dialogues agonize,
lose their wit,
its dreams
have lost their words
have crumbled
silence begins to reign.

The song
the birds' song
is slight and cold, its hymns
where shall we hear them again?

The air arrives in rags, exhausted
and late.

The rivers give us a bitter look
a look of despair.

The earth's entrails
intoxicated
exhale bad breath.

The plants
no longer sprout with strength
with yesterday's mirth.

Tomorrow, scared
with a pale face
and an undernourished body
runs the risk of aborting.

Tomorrow,
tomorrow is in danger
tomorrow
runs the risk of not arriving
ever again!

Tomorrow depends on us
So! it is essential
to recover the reason of our being
it is essential
to take care of its womb
make its birth
a normal birth
that its child be healthy
and vigorous
so that we all,
all will cuddle it
in our arms
baptize it
in the name of:
Humanity!

translated from Quechua (Kitchua) and
Spanish by Marisa Estelrich

Pachaka

Pachaka
tukyakuk shina
ashtaka ashtaka punkishkami kan
nanymanta, makita wichachishpa
samayta, kutin kutin kachashpa
junpisapa kaypi tiyakunmi.
Pachaka, makikunata ninanta chutachishpa
suyukunapi alli alli japirishpa
wakashpa, nanrishpa, junpisapa tuyakunmi.
Pachaka,
yawar sapa, yawarsapa tiyakun
nanaymanta
paskarinkapak kallarin
puchukay samyta, ima mutupash
lluksiechun sakin.

Pachaka
kay nanimanta
mushuk intita
mushuk killata
wachachinkapak
kallarishkami

El Tiempo

El tiempo
el tiempo está convulsionado
el tiempo, tiene contracciones
el tiempo, puja, aprieta sus puños
está bañado en sudor
el tiempo, extiende sus brazos
sus manos se crispan en las orillas del horizonte
¡suda, se queja, grita¡
sus dolores son mas intensos
el tiempo,
está extremadamente dilatado
el tiempo
comienza a romperse empieza a sangrar
el tiempo
deja escaper, su ultimo suspiro
un nuevo sol
una nueva luna
ha empezado
a nacer

Time

Time
time is not at rest
time has its contradictions
time pushes, clenches its fists
is soaked in sweat
time opens its arms
its hands tense on the horizon shores
it sweats, complains, screams!
its pain is deeper
time
is extremely dilated
time
begins to break
to bleed
time
lets out its last sigh
a new sun
a new moon
has begun
its birth.

> translated from Quechua (Kitchua) and
> Spanish by Marisa Estelrich

May Sumak Kayman

Ecuatormanta Yayakunaman, sinchi shayarishkamanta

Sinchi yuyaiwan kay kausayta,
wiñachinata usharkanchik
ñukanchik makiwan
kay pachata, kay kausayta wiñachishkamanta
ñukanchikta, mana, mana sarunata ushankachu

Chikita, ñukanchik ñakariwan
Takiwan, kallpachirkanchik
rupay juyaiwan
Shamuk pachakunata, wakaychirkanchik
Chaymanta, ñukanchiktaka, mana, mana
sarunata ushankakunachu

Ushak mana ushak kakpipash
Tukuy runakunapi asinata, shuyuchirkanchik
Chay asinata, ñukanchikmi pukuchinata usharkanchik
Ñukachik makimi pukuchinata usharkami
Chaymanta, ñukanchiktaka, mana, mana
sarunata ushankakunachu

Ñukanchipak muskuita
Ñukanchipak kayta kausachikuimanta
Kaypi kanchik, kaypi kanchik ninkapak
Shamushkanchik, kaypi kashun ninkapak
shamushkanchikmi
Chaymanta, ñukanchiktaka, mana, mana
sarunata ushankakunachu

Canto a la Dignidad

a los jubilados del Ecuador, en homenaje a su lucha

Porque con la vitalidad de nuestro pensamiento
Le dimos fondo, forma esta vida
Porque con nuestra illusion construimos
Los espacios, los sonidos, los gestos que nos rodean
No, no nos vencerán.

Porque con la fecundidad de nuestra ternura
los arrullos que ahuyentaron el espanto
El calor de nuestros brazos de volcaán
Abrigamos de seguridad y amor al futuro
No, no nos vencerán.

Porque a pesar de todo, la sonrisa que se dibuja
En el rostro del pueblo, es truto de nuestros largos recorridos,
de estas manos que hicieron florecer los campos áridos
que injertaron la sonrisa, la tranquilidad
en la desesperanza de nuestros hijos
No, no nos vencerán.

Por que nuestros sueños
aun sostienen el splendor de nuestra dignidad
estamos aquí, de pie y de manera
frontal para decirles cara a cara, con voz de trueno
y el puño en alto
No, no nos vencerán.

A Song to Dignity

> to the retired people of Ecuador, in honor of their struggle

Because with the vitality of our minds
We gave depth and form to this life.
Because with illusions we built
the spaces, the sounds, the gestures that surround us.
No, they will not defeat us.

Because of the fruitfulness of our love
The lullabies frightened off the horror.
With our arms of volcanic warmth
We sheltered their safety and love for the future
No, they will not defeat us.

Because in spite of it all, the smile appearing
In the faces of the people, is the fruit of our long travels
With these hands which transformed arid fields into flowers
grafted smiles, peacefulness
In the hopelessness of our sons
No, they will not defeat us.

Because our dreams
Still hold the splendor of our dignity,
We are here, standing up and facing them
To say face to face, with thundering voice and
Our fists raised
No, they will not defeat us.

> translated from Quechua (Kitchua) and
> Spanish by Graciela Lucero Hammer

Margaret Noori

Jim Northrup, "Ji-bmose Ishkonigan Miikan"

> To walk reservation road
> Walking the Rez Road

Gwedwin—Aaniidash aanind ininatigo-ziigwaagamide makadeagame
    miinwaa
Question Why some maple syrup   dark   and

aanind nangagame?
some   light

Question—Why is it that some maple syrup is dark and some is light?

Tkwedwin—Zaam enji dibikad aanind ndo'zaawaa.
Answer because in night some we boil them

Answer—Because some we boil at night.

Dibiki-Ziigwaagaame
    Night Syrup

Ziigwaagame n'daagwaagominaan
I stir syrup into

makademashkikiabo miinwaa
coffee   and

kwejimdizo,   "Wenesh e-naagamig
I ask myself   "What

dibikiziigwaagame?"
does night syrup taste like?"

Gete-misaabe-zekwekik ina?
The ancient iron kettle?

Giiwedinong giizhik ina?
Northern cedar?

Zagaswans ina?
A bit of smoke?

maage
or

Enangwiiganing aandeg ina?
The wing of a crow?

Moozo akiianzo shkiijigan ina?
The brown eye of a moose?

Shki miikans-maamad tigwaking ina?
A new path in the woods?

Ode noondan abita-dibikong ina?
Hearing a heart beat at midnight?

Miidash nsostooyaanh
And then I understand

wiishkobii-kade-aagamide
sweet   dark syrup

bimaadiziwin e-naagamig.
tastes like life.

Jim Northrup

Dash Iskigamiziganing

Nimbiindaakoojige,
Ninga-naadoobi iwidi noopiming wayiiba
Aaniin apii waa-ozhiga'igeyan iwidi Gwaaba'iganing dash,
Mii bijiinag i'iw apii baadaajimowaad aandegwag dash,
Mii zhigwa oshki-ziigwang
Aaniin dash apane wenji-izhichigeyan i'iw dash,
Apane nimishoomisiban apane gii-izhichige dash,
Awenen wii-wiidookawik iskigamizigeyan dash,
Indanawemaaganigdog miinawaa dash, niwiijiwaagan dash,
Awenen waa-mawadisik iskigamizigeyan dash,
Awegwen iidog dash,
Aaniin dash apane wenji-izhichigeyan dash,
Ninijaanisag miinawaa dash, noozhishenyag miiniwaa dash, akina
Anishinaabeg niigaan igo ani-nitaa-iskigamizigewag dash,
Awegonen waa-aabajitooyan iwidi iskigamiziganing dash,
Ninga-indaabaji'aa asema dash, ininaatigoog dash, bagone-igan dash,
Negwaakwaanan dash, ziinibaakwadwaaboo dash, iskigamiziganaak dash,
Okaadakik dash, misan dash, iskigamigani-ishkode dash, zhingobaandag
    dash, dibaajimowinan dash
Mii iw
Mii sa iw

title . . . *And at the sugar bush*

1. . . . I make an offering of tobacco
2. . . . Soon I will gather sap over there in the woods
3. . . . When will you tap trees over there in Sawyer and
4. . . . At the exact time when the crows arrive telling news and
5. . . . At the time of the new spring
6. . . . Why do you always do this and
7. . . . Always my dead grandfather always did this and
8. . . . Who will help you at your sugarbush and
9. . . . My relatives and my partner and
10. . . . Who will visit at your sugarbush and
11. . . . I don't know who and
12. . . . Why do you always do this
13. . . . I do it for my children and grandchildren and all
14. . . . Anishinaabeg so they will come to know how go to the sugarbush and
15. . . . What will you use over there at your sugarbush and
16. . . . I will use tobacco, and maple trees and a drill and
17. . . . Taps and maple sap and a frame for the boiling kettle and
18. . . . a kettle and firewood and a fire only for boiling sap and a balsam branch and stories and
19. . . . That's it
20. . . . That's really it.

The List We Make

Asani Charles

Grease

I like fried chicken with my frybread
cuz grease is grease
and that season salt chicken juice
sops up good on Indin bread.

I like black eyed peas in my corn stew
cuz peas swim good next to sweet corn
oh and
I get to choose,
hot water corn bread or blue corn cakes
dayum, that's good.

I love peaches and cream
with my frybread
cuz when grandma met grandpa
they got together and
made something good.

Now, if I can just fina
friedchickenfrybreadblackeyepeacornstew joint somewhere
half way between the rez and the 'hood,
dayum,
I'd be set.

Santee Frazier

Coin Laundry

Spinning washers. Whirr of dryers. Soda machine humming.
Baskets on hips, underneath chairs and tables. The infant,
boy or girl, head on its mother's chest, cradled by the nape.
The mother ties knots on each shoulder, strapping the infant to her,
in a carrier too rough-hewn and tattered to have been store bought.
On the edge of sleep, gnawing at its knuckle, the infant
must be teething, crying in the early morning hours when the darkness
is thinning, the sky dim as shade. She puts a slice of apple
to its mouth; the infant refuses and looks to her other shoulder.
Its thin hair, light brown, undulating, through and around
its mother's long, wood-brown fingers. Until that one last coo,
the coo of sleep, the light push of the infant's chest.
Spinning washers. Whirr of dryers. Soda machine humming.
Baskets on hips, underneath chairs and tables. The infant
boy or girl, still sleeping, ear over the mother's heart
as if still in the womb, kicks once, twice. Pre-wash and spin.
Wash and spin. Rinse and spin. The mother's hands in and out of washers,
her pocket of quarters swaying with her hips as she wheels
her clothes to the dryer, one hand still on the nape, one hand on the cart.
The clank of metal on metal, quarters dropping, the dryers revving to start.
Spinning washers. Whirr of dryers. Soda machine humming.
Baskets on hips, underneath chairs and tables. The infant
boy or girl, stretching out its arms, balls its hands, gazes
up at its mother's shoulders tensing as she shifts the carrier higher
on her chest and re-offers the apple. Its small mouth sucking her finger
and the apple as if there is no difference between them, its mouth and her finger,
its mouth and the apple. The mother swaying one leg to the other,
grabbing a skirt, then folding. The infant still strapped to her, whimpering
for the apple, hands pushing at her chest, her lean arms gently
placing the clothes in a basket. One last shift of carrier, she lines up the basket
on her hip, with the other leans on the door, hand on the infant's nape, swings it

open.

Cross-Town

> Where they sell you grease in a box, and hope that
> you die quicker, and if you're old enough to walk
> to the store you can buy liquor.
> —*Masta Ace*

Downtown. Transit Station. Trail-pipes and exhaust.
      Bus 8, bus 6, cross-town, 3rd, 16th, the bus swaying,
         then stopping. As the riders step out into the glum,
      dead-beat day, greasy, thick, and gray, and the dingy air
crawls from the door to my seat—I think of the time
      my father's hands tightened around my throat
        and face. How from the off-white wall,
      my legs dangled, and he slung me to the floor.
I could not read it, the work that got me beaten

      and bloody. Sounding it out *rah-ing*—
        knocked upside my head for not knowing
      what I was spelling meant, *r-i-n-g*. I step onto the grid,
Western Avenue, where on either side
      of the road the guts of houses still stand rickety
        on their foundations. Work still 6 blocks,
      on the corner of 23rd, where inside
I flip burgers, clean grease traps,
      and mop floors. Two blocks, through an alley,

      craggy-shattered bottles of Mickey's, the smell
      of urine. I see a mutt, its coat almost cinder-gray, mangy
at the tail and neck, sniffing its way through a bag
      of trash it must have gnawed open with its teeth.
        The scavenger barked as I rounded the bend.
      Making my way to NW 23rd, a store—
every window barred, folks out front, posted up
      on the wall, paper-bagged bottles in hand.
        I walk to a cooler of beer and find the tallest,

cheapest can of rotgut. Rattle of change,
the beeping door, back out on 23rd. Twilight,
    90 degrees, some kids shirtless licking
        Red Bomber popsicles, ice cream truck
    chiming its way up the block. As I make
my way through MacArthur Park, I remember
    the time, amidst an onslaught of lights,
        the cops found a teenager in the parking-
    lot dumpster shot through this dome.

How do I sound it out, even still, dreading
    a barrage of blows, coming after every misread
        word? How do I spell, grease popping
    up from the grill and onto my face and hands?
On break, cigarette hanging from my lips,
    wheeling a load of soggy-bagged trash to the dumpster.
        I heard it was a kid from a few blocks over,
    the gunman a mystery. I remember his mother
at the scene almost weeping.

Nick Cheater

I done dropped that tranny,
    wrenched on that thang least till supper time,

didn't have no luck neither.
    Hell, that ratchet set I had was slippery as a dang ol perch.

Was up in grease tah my ears
    that one day I was rippin the engine block out mah Trans-am.

Ain't seen that ol station wagon
    yah had, that ol burgundy one with gold trim.

You reckon that Buick up dah road
    is fur sale still? I thank he ought to let it go for bout

seven, eight hundred, shit,
    last I shot-the-shit with him, he told me 750 and one ah mah dogs.

Your car still make that funny noise
    when you rev up in the mornins? You might need tah get

you intake checked, hell,
    your head gasket might even be makin you car sound like at.

Told yah not tah get your car fixed in town,
    they thank since they got all em machines they know everythang.

Ol Marty Jumper took his Chevy
    over tah Good Wrench, they charged him double I woulda.

Natalie Diaz

Black Magic Brother

My brother's shadow flutters from his shoulders, a magician's cape.
My personal charlatan glittering in woofle dust
and loaded
with gimmicks and gaffs.

A train of dirty cabooses, of once-beautiful girls,
follows my magus man like a chewed tail
helping him perform his tricks.
He calls them his *Beloveds,* his *Sim Sala Bimbos,* juggles them,
shoves them into pipes packed hot hard as cannons and *Wham Bam
Ala-Kazam!* whirls them to smoke.
Sometimes he vanishes their teeth then points his broken wand up
into the starry desert sky,
says *Voila! There they are!*
and the girls giggle, revealing neon gums and purple throats.

My brother. My mago.
The consummate professional, he is dependable—performs daily,
nightly, in the living room, a forever-matinee, an always-late-shaman-show:
Come one come all! Behold the spectacle
of the Prince of Prestidigitators pulling wild animals from a hole
in his crotch—
you thought I'd say *hat,* but you don't know my black magic brother—
and those animals love him like the first animals loved God
when He gave them names.

My brother. Our perpetual encore—
he riddles my father with red silk scarves before sawing him in half
with a steak knife.
Now we have two fathers, one who weeps anytime he hears the word
Presto!
The other who drags his feet down the hall at night.
Neither has the stomach for steak anymore.
My mother, too, is gone somewhere
in one of the pockets of my brother's bluest tuxedo.

The audience is we—we have the stubs to prove it—
and we have been here for years, in velvet chairs the color of wounds,
waiting for something to fall,
maybe the curtain, maybe the crucifix on the wall,
or, maybe the pretty white doves my brother made disappear—
Now we see them, now we don't—
will fall from his sleeves like angels,
Right before our very eyes.

Why I Hate Raisins

> Is it only the mouth and belly that are injured by hunger?
> —*Mencius*

Love is a pound of sticky raisins
packed tight in black and white
government boxes the day we had no
groceries. I told my mom I was hungry.
She gave me the whole bright box.
USDA stamped like a fist on the side.
I ate them all in ten minutes. Ate
too many too fast. It wasn't long
before those old grapes set like black
stones at the bottom of my belly
making it ache and swell.

I complained *I hate raisins.*
I just wanted a sandwich like other kids.
Well that's all we've got my mom sighed
And what other kids?
Everyone but me I told her.
She said *You mean the white kids.*
You want to be a white kid?
Well too bad cause you're my kid.
I cried *At least the white kids get a sandwich.*
At least the white kids don't get the shits.

That's when she slapped me. Left me
holding my mouth and stomach. Left me
to be devoured by shame.

To this day I hate raisins.
Not for the crooked commodity lines
we stood in to get them—winding
around and in the tribal gymnasium.
Not for the awkward cardboard boxes
we carried them home in. Not for the shits
or how they distended my belly.
I hate raisins because now I know
my mom was hungry that day too
and I ate all the raisins.

Marcie R. Rendon

My Child's Hunger . . .

my child's hunger keeps me company
working all night
fingers turned raw from spools of thread wound too tight
trying to gain an extra yard
from a spool of thread not meant to stretch that far
my children's future stitched into high-fashion seams
working all night
an extra dollar made

my child's hunger keeps me company
working all night
in an outfit made
from spools of thread wound too tight
a soul's not meant to stretch this far
in too-tight
too-high
high-heeled shoes.
slipping off the edge of the world
is what i do best
working all night
an extra dollar made

aching bodies
sell dreams
exchanging expendable commodities
for an extra dollar made

working evening shifts
graveyard time/midnight dust
holds dreams alive

Foster Care Blues Cont.

Rock and roll beats
Juxtaposed on jingle dress songs

I never learned to move my feet
To a gentle heartbeat
Adrenalin rush
Fight or flight

Throwing left-hooks
Duck
Dip to the right
Sugar Ray shuffle
Muhammad Ali
butterfly beat
My medicine dance
Was a warrior dance
Avoiding blows
I had more than one
Rope-a-dope
Fight

Security

my mother wrapped her legs around my father
hoping for security from a world gone mad
my mother wrapped her legs around John Deere and Massey Ferguson
hoping to ride out the drought of a red river valley summer
and drunken farmers grabbing milk-laden breasts
my mother fought her demons as best she could
two fists
fired into iron will over the hot coals of extermination
she fought and fought
her love disappeared into red hot rage
wrapping her legs around the world
she ran into the vast expanse of Montana stillness
no mountain range could hold her
she ran
until the breath from her lungs burst out
and screamed into the never-ending sky
her legs tired
worn out
she sleeps
and returns to river banks
and wild rice lakes
guarding great-grandchildren
while they dream
of generations yet to come

Luke Warm Water

Wani`cokan wi
    (Moon of Middle Winter)

Just before sunrise this morning
crows land on the tall oak trees outside my bedroom
kaw-kaw for a few minutes before flying away
trying to take the memory of my dream

Last night I dreamt of an old man hunched over
wearing shabby clothes brown wrinkled face
white chin whiskers
long thick salt and pepper hair with a black feather in it

Old man drinks from a bottle and says
wana`gi wana`gi ghosts ghosts
wa yan ka wa yan ka look look
he takes another drink wiping his wet chin whiskers
opens his worn out brown corduroy coat
dry heaving *wana`gi wana`gi, wa yan ka wa yan ka*
his gaunt torso is deformed
his body is a map of North America
from the Aleutian Islands to Key West
I look closer, his body is covered with ticks
but they are not ticks
they are the souls of the lost

Old man takes another drink and says
wana`gi wana `gi, wa yan ka wa yan ka
the lost souls on his torso move about
screaming, sobbing, laughing maniacally

Old man closes his corduroy coat
fast and tight to his taut rib cage
setting the bottle on the ground
to a thunderous glass concrete clink

I walk away slow hunched over
rubbing my white chin whiskers
then running my crooked fingers through
my long salt and pepper hair
touching my black feather
pulling my corduroy coat tight to me
mumbling to myself inaudible to my dream
mouthing *ghosts ghosts look look*

Waking before the murder of crows
fly off from the oaks
to kaw-kaw and take away
the haunting of this dream

Reale Redlance

Storm Forest King

I knew what was coming all along, I watched with awesome enthrallment in my heart as magnetic fire sundered the sky and birthed blue clouds into the black night, white hot star strike lightning in the night smashed peace out of the cosmos above me, dust and water electric elementals danced frigid fear and lonely tear drops from on high into my empty field. I loved the moon truly, but I believed in a brighter light still, the rain made me cold and brittle. Dare to find me there freezing, and I would find a way to warm you yet. Cut myself to gift you a single moment of the heat hidden under my icy flesh. I loved the teeming grass but in the hot uncertain solar wind I could not plant seeds, and know them to be certainly fruitful, iron titanic tall and proud. day break is coming and I have grown a forest to shield me from sun fire fury as I travel unto your lonely field.

Gabriela Spears Rico

Eulogy for Ramona

In the lacandon jungle
they will bury Ramona:
Tzotzil woman
daughter of mother earth
granddaughter of the moon
sister to the animals and trees

In southeast Mexico
they will bury Ramona:
insurgent commander
Zapatista sister
idealist woman
who gave birth to a revolution

In the wet mountains of Chiapas
they will bury Ramona.
. . . over there, where the government
isolated Indians to separate them from 'civilization'

Over there, *en los altiplanos*
they will bury Ramona
so our ancestors may welcome her
in the Spirit World
so Totilme'il, the Great Creator
will receive her in his arms

Last night, Mayan communities
formed a circle around a fire
drinking the warm juice
of guayabas and sugar cane
while they held vigil
over little bitty Ramona
warrior woman
who passed away.

Historical experts, politicians
and economists have continuously proclaimed
these modern times of globalization
neo-colonization
and endless violence
would wipe out
the people of copper.

We'd get lost in time
amidst genocide and extinction.

But I know,
women crafted from clay
emerge from the center of earth;
we grow among corn-stalks
forever safe in the mother's sacred embrace.

I remember them—
Tzotzil artisans
earning their right to live
in tourist Veracruz—
and they, too, knew about you
Ramona
they sold keychains
with your image for *ten pesos*
reminding us it's the heart
which carries resistance.

In the lacandon jungle
in southeast Mexico
on the lush Chiapanecan mountains
they will bury Ramona

and what will remain, I ask myself?
What will remain of Ramona?
Short indigenous woman
with the power to command
thousands of troops of men
with one slanted look of her eyes.

What will remain of the commander
whose six words
mobilized an entire nation?
"Never again, a Mexico without us"
from where I am, I repeat them . . .

What will remain of the vulnerable, benevolent,
un-invincible, loving Ramona?
Will only her replicas remain?

Zapatista dolls
faces hidden behind red bandanas and ski masks
rifles strapped across their breasts?
adorning Chicano altars
or keychains hanging from backpacks?

What **will** remain
are the whispers
of her spirit
traveling amidst the four winds
forever speaking hidden codes
of struggle and liberation.

Strawberry Hands

skin so dry
scorched by
the fires of
a thousand suns

so dry
that Tlaloc's rain
can't even saturate
the peeling pain away

slits carefully
carved into
wholesome
brown flesh
soaked in the redness
of strawberry juice
until those hands
are so bruised
your babies are
scared of your caress

rough like
the texture of
papier-mâché
criss-cuts of *picadillo*
trails of skin cells
scattered upon
lush strawberry fields:
live farmworker DNA

deformed and crooked
those hands cry out
to contratistas
who never pay

Yet proud and dignified,
they hold up picket signs
demanding water breaks
            a living wage.

"Soon, those poor
hands will get arthritis,"
your worried mother says.

But for today
they thrive
      you think
feed five
hungry mouths
and pay the rent

those hands that strive
hands that love
hands that die
and never, ever once complain

mamá's hands
tio's hands
a Mixtec client's hands at an office
in Central Califas, CRLA

. . . so bent and crooked
that I can't help
but be amazed

at hands that struggle
hands that fight
hands survive
Farm-worker:
Creator bless the simple
beauty of your hands.

Carolyn Dunn

Mvskoke Giveaway
for Joy

All the things
One needs for survival
In this foreign
But known home country.
Horses,
In power of 6,
Cooking pots,
Fire for warmth,
And Christmas wrapping paper.
Do you know
What we have become?
Travelers
Like seed
On a space of wind
Strewn by clan mothers
And the sea
To where we
Become
Survivors.
Glass shards
And pieces of bone,
Born
In spaces of land, sea,
Air
To ride horses
In powers of six.
It's a good thing.
Gold for the journey home
To the place of emergence.
Manna from heaven
And a piece left behind
In a place where
Roots should be.

Nothing remains,
Hidden lives
That speak the cost of sorrow,
Grief.
Grief that shatters bone,
Kills the mind slowly
Until one day
There is nothing
Left but flesh
And blood.
Blood ties to this land
When one grieves for
Tall trees
And at angle of flight.
The memory stays
But for the briefest touch
And to the land
Ride horses
In the power of 6
Speaking to the clan
Of the One Who Left.
Things of survival
This way
Migrating across the sea
Scattered seeds
Are sown
And we remain
In all places
Pieces left along
A trail
Marked with
Bone and blood
Bread and salt
Red earth and tears
Deer and horses
In the power of 6
To call us
Home.

Gordon D. Henry

Simple Four Part Directions for Making Indian Lit

Ah-Beshig for the money:
Take something Indin
and take something
non
Indin
Make the indin
indigenous or native
or skin

Make the
non
indin
non
indigenous or
non
native
or non
skin
or white

Ah-Two for the shonyaa:
Make the indin non indin
And the non indin indin
Or the white indin

Ah-T(h)ree:
Make a character out of paper
Write a name with fire
or sky, or a combination of
color and the names of birds
or the absence of an article
with a present tense verb
from a limited number of infinitives

(you may) include prepositions,
except: forego, between, beyond, under
over, into, across, beside, beneath;
avoid abstractions, slang, economic terms,
hip phrases, or contemporary
situations or signs.

(You cannot use, for example, the names

foregoes hawk
under crow
into deer
Values Dog
Or Love Crane
Or Dances Similar
Or In the Middle of Night
red thunder banging
or
Across wolf
Eating Horse
Bling Eagle
or Has in Trust
or Many Shoes
or Sun Dude
or Chick Lit
or Donut Shop
Yard Sale Man
Beneath the Ground
Upside the Head
Do not Cross
or Out of Position
or Big Credit
or Bear Pimp
or Stone Suitcase
or Ice Cream Turtle
or Calls the Taxi
or Waits for Bus
or Bums a Smoke

or Speaks the Bible
Running Mascara
or Saint Muskrat
or Graffiti Cloudsor Air Flute
or Telescope Woman
or Medicine Cheese
or Karma Bull
or Missus Layups
or Nice One
or Red Exit
or Off Limits
Or even
Working Man)

So, maybe take a break
offer prayers to the polytheistic
Indo European Spirits
of syntax

inscribe a smoke or a ceremony

Add laughter to fighting
Tears to anything
sounding like history
Reinscribe Indian
Non Indian
White

Repeat

Imperialism
   conquest
Imperialism disease medicine
   conquest alcohol
Imperialism guns bow
   conquest
Imperialism

Make crossing tongues
As simple as pow wow for profit
And dying chevy hey yaw
As complex as Aristotle remains ethical
And remains remain catalogued
Use newspapers, magazines, museum brochures,
Skatagon, flint and match
Roll characters, names words, onto paper
Paper into rolls
Rub with beargrease and lard,
Or last night's ground beef leavings
(this will not work with
Olive or sunflower oil)
Say four hail marys, a couple of
Aho's or ah ah kaweekin
Ignite all of the above

Ah-Forza:

After all this becomes lit
Be careful about who you
Read to

They may be hearing
Indin in everything
Non Indin

(As what remains from fire is not spirit)

LeAnne Howe

The List We Make

Part 1

First Note:
America is 82 percent Christian. 60 percent of the population believes the Bible is historical fact. The President of the United States has endorsed Jesus as his favorite philosopher.

Second Note:
From today's perspective, cannibalism among early Indians appears to have had a greater stringency than was actually the case. The inclination of history to list these incidents creates the impression that opposing groups simply ate each other as a way of ending conflict. We did not have the aim of discovering cannibalism, but discovering what was in us. . . .

Third Note:
As Catherine Albanese has shown, Anglo-American literature transformed Davy Crockett from a frontier settler and soldier into a violent superhero communing with the overwhelming spirit of the wilderness by killing and eating bears and Creek Indians.

Fourth Note:
Luis and Salvadore, the two Miwok guides for the infamous Donner Party, were the first to be shot and eaten. For many American Indians, Luis and Salvadore represent us all:

William Foster, a keen tracker of red blood had become deranged, and it is understandable why, knowing what he endured. He was terrified he would die from starvation, and Foster planned on murdering the Indians for food. Eddy, a friend told Luis and Salvadore, who promptly ran away. The party followed the tracks of Luis and Salvadore. It was easy. The feet of the Indians had become so raw from exposure all their toes had fallen off, marking their trail with blood. Foster figured if the Indians didn't lead them to safety, they could at least find their corpses to use as food.

By January 9th or 10th, the Indians had suffered terrible exposure to the cold, and had survived on practically nothing to eat, with no fire. They couldn't last like that. They gave out near a small creek, and it was here the Forlorn Hope came upon them. Despite arguments from some and the Indians' look of terror, Foster shot the two Indians with his rifle. Though they would not have lived long, the act was horrifying.

Part 2
The waiting road
arrives
this time San Francisco
moves along the abyss
in a black car filled with dawn and
men's underwear.

Again,
a membrane binds us
I crave all you offer
your hands,
your poet's wrists that bleed
on the page
your penis of words
that penetrates my vagina
like a wet weapon.

We drape our bodies with new surroundings,
like moveable sets on a theater stage
we fear hammer and nails,
hunger,
death,
longing,
and consumption.

We café
trying to remember who we are,
for each other, I mean
at Dolly's, wide omelets,
big cups of brown Espresso unearth
old hungers, centuries old
beckon.

"Yes," curves us together
and we breathe in the same thin air
We breathe in each other
And forget all that has happened.

On the road made flesh
they separated us
from our fingers and toes
separated us from our bones.
At first, we are swallowed whole
like the wafers of God
down the gullets of hungry Christians.
Everything we did, everything we didn't do
is digested in their dreams
Now they know us better than we knew ourselves

On the lam (again) we head north into the mountains
becoming what we fear, consumers of goods and services.
We give twenty dollars to a stranger
to teach us how
to attach the chains so
we can slip past Donner Pass
where banquet chairs pose
still as icicles
patiently awaiting our return.

We race toward the Biltmore Motel
Our music is hard sevens
We lunch in the high Sierras and
You teach me to gamble.
We crash a writer's conference
A bad poet reads an 'ode to appetite'
But this time we will not be dinner.

Part 3

Seven thousand feet up
though Lake Tahoe stalks us
we practice our escape by devouring a
repugnant pig like our captors once devoured us.
At the All American Café
you in grey to my conventional black
we dine on goose liver,
pineapple, and curried ice cream.
Where are Luis and Salvadore now?
Who the hell cares! We're following
a treasure map of flesh and blood
The ghost camouflage of exotic appetites
that came for Luis and Salvadore,
has infected us all.
And,
what of this steamy you and I?
This steam
This you and I
Imprisoned by a hoary God's ravenous hunger
We have not shadow's gaze
Nor eyes and ears.
No shadowy past.
Nothing but poetry
made manifest within a complexion of stars
Our bodies
Geometry now
Conjoined in the heavens
On earth as
Luis y Salvadore
Conjoined in blood,
And oddly enough
Love.

Brunoe

How Many Aubades Have Passed This Year Alone?

*for Agha Shahid Ali, "I will die that day in late October,
it will be long ago"*

1.

And I remember this every morning,
like today, as I wake up hung over
and walk to the aroma-filled bathroom
of yesterday's piss. I leave the toilet un-
flushed, walk past today's additional bottles
of Dahlwinnie, Oban, and Talisker; the replacements
of fine China you took; past the peeling wallpaper
floral patterned both pink and blue, and into
the kitchen. It's the one place I reclaimed: I cook
sausage, ham, and bacon with eggs and toast,
use my right arm to flip the food, and then I
remind myself: that vegetarian shit you cooked made me soft.
Though, I find it funny that I now garden. I quit
work to become a self-employed landscaper.
I garden my own: roses, of course, both white and red,
a long line of Irises, some Dahlias, and others.
One morning last spring I found a Snap
Dragon wilted, bit by a late frost, slouching
like the head and shoulders of a boy child
told to do a task or chore. My right hand gripped the stem,
pulled it by the roots from the ground. I leave only the living.

2.

Although I will not die that day in late October, so long ago,
my left arm remains limp early mornings—as if that boy child
in me remains behind on a Sunday evening walk, tugging at it
for me to slow down—numb to the fact that you're now gone:

> It's a nifty trick
> I learned some years ago,
> place the cleft of my chin
> on the middle of my bicep,
> dig in, and sleep,
> dig in, and sleep.

Tessa Mychael Sayers

New Lessons

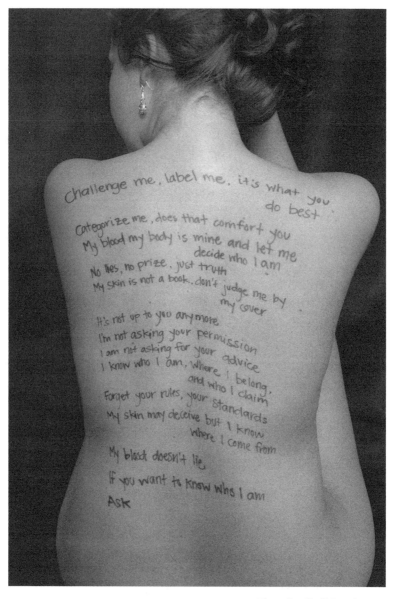

Challenge me, label me, it's what you do best
Categorize me, does that comfort you
My blood my body is mine and let me decide who I am
No lies, no prize, just truth
My skin is not a book, don't judge me by my cover

It's not up to you anymore,
I'm not asking your permission
I am not asking for your advice
I know who I am, where I belong, and who I claim
Forget your rules, your standards
My skin may deceive but I know where I come from

My blood doesn't lie,
If you want to know who I am
Ask

Photo by Chad Braithwaite

Richard Van Camp

Stolen Poem

Hey hey
You see that woman over there?
That's my wife.
I took her to the Sundance last summer, thank you very much.
She let me dance close this time
And the last time she looked east
it rained . . .

Calendar for the folks from my hometown of Fort Smith, NWT

as compiled by Richard Van Camp

May–June

Ice Breaking Up Time

- Trapping muskrats for food and fur
- In May, there is a Salt River run of suckers.
- Hunt for porcupine and beaver
- Cut and peel logs
- You can pick plants for medicine like spruce gum and rat root.
- Collect birch bark for baskets, canoes
- Bird hunting (grouse, ptarmigan). Some of us do it all year round!
- NHL Playoffs!
- The little red Buffalo calves are born
- Wolves are raising their pups in their dens
- Caribou cows lose their antlers after the calves are born

June–August

When the Water and Sun are Warm

- Waterways open during June.
- Beaver hunters return to their families and after the Treaty payments honouring the Treaty 8 and Treaty 11 payment of 1899 and 1921 respectively. Everybody has a good time.

- National Aboriginal Day on June 21st, eh. Take a break and give'er! Tan hides
- Make hide teepees
- Forest Fire season.
- Strawberries are good in July.
- You can try mooching fresh strawberry jam from your granny's house!
- Nobody hunts in the summer. That is when the animals have their little ones. It's their time to be a family.
- In late June and early August, women prepare dry fish while the men go hunting
- Gather plants, roots, berries, spruce gum, tamarack bark
- Canoe building
- Some people start making dry meat.
- High bush cranberries and Saskatoon berries are ready at the end of July. Don't wait too long or they will dry up.
- This is the best weather for fishing in the Slave River. The best time for fishing in the lakes is when the ice goes out in the spring and in the fall before freeze up. The lakes turn over (that means they circulate from top to bottom) and the big trout come up into shallower water from down in the deeps.
- When the wolf pups get too frisky for their dens, they get moved to rendezvous sites and then start moving around with the adults.
- By the middle of the summer the buffalo calves start turning from red to brown. By the end of August only the late calves are still red.
- By the middle of August the buffalo rut is on. They move around and get into larger groups. They are most likely to hang around near the highways and get into trouble with the traffic.

August–September

When it Gets Darker

- Pick your berries. Cranberries are great in September.
- Make dry meat for sure as there's no flies.
- Northern lights come back to us for the winter
- The cool weather is perfect to make dry fish
- Geese hunting in September.
- Low bush cranberries are ready in September.

- People hunt bears to make grease before they go in the hole in late September when they're just fat!
- Wolf pups that are too small get left behind by their packs. The big strong pups run with the adults and start learning how to hunt.
- Buffalo calves have to be able to keep up with their mothers. The cow and calf groups break into smaller herds and start moving to winter ranges. Red calves are rare; most have turned dark brown like the adults.
- Caribou and Moose antlers are in velvet.

September–October

When the Wind Gets Cold/When the Moose Meets its Mate

- The rut's on so start hunting moose.
- Richard Van Camp's birthday on September 8th. Virgo, hey.
- The NHL starts around the first of October!
- Make snowshoes, toboggans, toboggan bags and dog harnesses.
- Duck and geese hunting in September before they fly south.
- Blueberries are good from September to freeze up when they get frost. Then they fall off.
- The small, weak wolf pups die.
- Buffalo hides get thick and then they grow their full winter coat.
- Caribou start moving back into the trees.

October–February

Freeze Up

- Get your wood for the long winter.
- Trapping (squirrel, weasel, mink, fox, wolf, lynx, wolverine, beaver, marten, otter)
- The wolves are busy trying to catch calves or corner older buffalo that get left behind by their herds. Sometimes they will even go after prime bulls. It might take days or weeks to wound and finally kill their prey.
- The buffalo are busy pushing snow out of the way with their huge faces so they can feed on the green sedges that are frozen under the snow in the wet meadows. When the wolves get too bothersome they might move long distances to get away.
- Caribou rut in late November and the bulls lose their antlers around Christmas time.

November–February

When the Days are Short

- In the third week of December, the moose start losing their antlers
- Ptarmigan and wild chicken hunting
- Travel by dogs
- Make trail by snowshoe
- Trapping
- You can snare rabbits
- You use up your woodpile and the kids play video games by the woodstove. (Um, my dad sent this one in . . .)
- The smoke rises straight up from the chimneys.

March–April

When the Days are Long

- Caribou camp. Hunt those barren land caribou
- Ptarmigan hunting
- Ice fishing (with hooks)
- Trapping muskrat from March to the middle of May before the season closes.
- In the olden days, men would go to the fort in April and May to sell fur. As the ice melted, they left for spring beaver and a muskrat hunt. The hunters went from their toboggans to their canoes.
- End of March, baby wolverines are born.
- In April, the caribou start migrating to their calving grounds
- The pregnant caribou cows start to show. They only have a month or so to get to the calving grounds and have their new calves.

Please keep in mind that George Jones is always in season!

Michael Running Wolf Jr.

I Chased You

In an amber field, I tried to intercept your frantic path,
but all my speed, cursing, and pleading did nothing,
you were soon a plume of dust beyond any notice of me
dejected, I sat in silence as two of my closest friends approached,
two butterflies lost in a particularly complex breeze

the butterflies proposed I swoop down in front of you
they declared I do so with a flight of eagles
they demanded I land with thunder in my toes

bewildered, I wandered among the evidence of your passing,
dimples in the prairie and echoes of rabbit laughter

the rabbits whispered your latest good news
they whimpered you're the newest tragedy
they screamed your latest joke

lonelier, I ran amidst a family gathering dust from the grey air,
a tribe of buffalo spooked by news of a cousin in jail

the buffalo, without asking me, filled my lungs with dusty giggles
they gave me a laugh that startles grass in far away valleys
they forced me to swallow a rolling hoof born boom

confident, I sought knowledge among pits of fat prairie dogs
they pointed chubby arms at hills that smelled like yucca
the prairie dogs also told me I should build a great house first
they showed me how to stay warm for months at a time
they taught me that the secret was in how you hold one another
finally, I find you sitting atop a hill, quietly talking to an audience
of dandelions, turnips, and shy gophers
I try not to let my feet sparkle with butterfly magic
as I restrain the buffalo charge echoing in my chest
and, without rabbit wit or prairie dog wealth, I say hi

Donna Beyer

Weetigo

he lived in our basement

with its javex stained floor
and peculiar pink walls

behind the old furnace
where the black ball bobbed
and crickets kept secrets

at night
he would stir

hands first
dragging his crippled body behind him up the greyed wooden stairs
the bridge between his world and mine

each plank creaked
and rusty nails screamed

the door would open
and its hinges shriek
as his white haired head appeared

the wheels of a velvet plush chair would screech
as he slithered on its seat

and he would sit and he would roll
that weetigo
in our basement

backroads

you become accustomed to their ride
black ice winters, washboard summers
your driving accommodates their form

bearings blown
shocks shot

lonely dogs linger
signs falter

hollow cans line their ditches sporadically
their contents now inside someone's nameless void

their potholes
the size of moon craters
giant bruises turned inward

her hands

the sink was starting to separate from its mount
due to the countless leans by those peering into the mirror above it
a mirror tinged with rust along its edges but served its purpose

with her hands
she fills the sink with warm water
she plops a baby soap bar inside, its smell is comforting
she swishes a stringy facecloth in the now foggy water, wringing it,
    soaking it

gently, she begins to wash my nisto year old face
i breathe it in

give me your hands
her hands cup mine, she rolls mine into hers
the warmth of the water, the comforting smell, and the softness of these
    hands, lull me
my little body begins to sway, comforted by these hands
gran's hands

hands of the only girl with many brothers
hands that buried nÌso husbands, but loved only one
hands that raised Èyin·yÈw children
hands that self taught to read and spell
hands that scrubbed little clothes and washed dirty floors
hands that skinned a w·pos and made its soup
hands that rolled bread and buttered bannock
hands that dipped cotton pudding bags each Christmas
hands that stitched, patched, and darned
hands that once told me her beautiful Cree words were that of a 'dumb
    Indian'
hands that warned me nuhmuh moniyas
hands that teased me
hands that never drank nor smoked
hands of faith

she is my gran
and these are her hands

Janet McAdams

Blessing the Americans

Bless the girl you buried beneath the fountain.
Bless the moment you might have changed your mind.
Bless the neighbor who heard nothing and the one who heard something
    and wanted to call for help and the one who heard something and
    called for help.

Bless the boys who longed for regret
instead of terror.
Bless the father's rifle
still at home
or in a backpack carried through school doors
but still unused
or in a locker latched with indecision.
Bless the wood that split or was too knotty
to be shaped to the stock of a rifle
Bless the metal not forged, the hand still open.
Bless October and June, when it didn't happen.
Bless the fingers that have not yet touched it.
the arm that does not lift it.
Bless the ones who said good morning.
Bless the ones who didn't.

Bless the girl who drank and lay down
in snow and slept. Bless the friend
who could not find her.
Bless the boy hiding from the bullies.
Bless the one punished for love,
for desire hardening between his legs
who tried to turn his loneliness, who tried to turn it.
Bless the girl who went back for her sweater and so
just missed the yellow bus, and the boy
lighting up behind Kroger and planning his day without lessons.
And bless the one who hid behind the heavy library table and the one
who thought to bolt the door and hand them one by one out the window.

Bless the red boy who wanted to be white.
Bless the boy who said I'll do anything and lived and the boy who said No
    and didn't.
Bless the girl sleeping beneath a fountain or buried
in the yard behind the trailer. Bless the one who went hiking. And the one
    who wanted
to marry and the one who was tired and took a ride rather than walk the
    one more mile home on a certain Wednesday.

Bless the air, the ground, the new grass bending beneath the heels of her
    brown shoes, each blade as it stands back up, forgetting her passing.
Bless the white oak splitting in the storm, the hill behind it, the life it led,
    the lightning-blessed wood we gather and take away.

Russell Square Station

Before we got lost I dreamed
we lay in a clean bed and you curled
warm as an animal around me.

I put my hands on the small hard apples
of your breasts. And dreamed about
sleeping like this and dreamed

we got lost in the subway and took
the wrong stairs when the people
who lived in the station's shadows

came out of the shadows and one
pushed a dead hand into my hand
and the last light went out

so it was dark, as dark
as it might be after fire or storm
or the imagined disasters

of the twenty-first century.
I wanted never to be lost there
or alone or in the crowded elevator

I knew could stop on any floor.
Before we got lost you sometimes
smelled of apples or at least

the warm air that covered your body
was its own orchard. I wanted
never to be lost along the 300

steps climbing out of Russell Square Station.
I wanted never to feel the hand
that held my hand in the dark

disaster of living like this.
alone and climbing out
or alone and not climbing.

Rain C. Goméz

Old Crawdad the Fisherman

It is said the Crawfish people were roped, netted and dragged to the surface. And so through water, mud, clay in shades of gray we rose to the shore, buoyant bayou blood. The gray earth opening turning orange it bled, red clay banks bursting, relinquishing us from shadows and water. We gather on bayou banks. How much mud do you hold in your claws Grandfather? Let me build a life with it.

I can't remember the
Last time I danced in the arms of anyone.
I hate remembering it was you.
Crouching in the corner
Weeping are the memories
Of lost loves.

I am brought to remember the stories of the Sufi poets, who sang in whirlwind to their *Beloved. Beloved,* no physical lover, no tangible body to warm, to roll to sink back into red banks, the warmth of water.

Your language is fluid
It slips around and over
Takes the shape of any container.
Natural dams breaking borders
Into greenish gray waters.

Grandfather my sister and I sing the song you taught, sitting on your porch all those years ago, we still sing to old grandfather crawdad. We weave baskets of pine straw. We weave baskets of cane. Grandfather moves in pattern, flowing ever outward, claws offering earthen memory. And we dive and rise continuously from waters pushed from the Gulf of Mexico into the interior deltas. Our inherited blood brackish as these bayous . . . neither fresh nor sea-salt; yet natural in its inherent Louisiana topography.

Carter Revard

Aesculapius Unbound[1]
(Ovid and Darwin in Oklahoma)

By beautiful design, a snake's jawbones
unhinge, so it can swallow
things bigger around
than it is.
I wondered, when
the old man shot a blacksnake in
the hen-house, then held it
up by the tail,
just how in hell those great big lumps
along its six-foot length, slow-twisting up and
down as it hung, had ever been
choked down.
Later, I heard that snakes
are deaf, those three hinged bones
had not yet turned into the malleus, incus
and stapes of my middle ear,
they have no tympanum
and no cochlea,
no auditory nerve, their brain only
processes earth's vibrations, but not thunder's,
so snakes don't sing, although perhaps
they dance when mating—
only their cousins, the small birds,[2]
sing the light's changes,
as Melampous knew.[3]

So when I heard,
as twilight grew, the orchard
oriole sing its heart out there in the elm's
green heaven, something unhinged
and let the music in,
but if they hold me up and listen,
it may by then be part of me—
be how I live and breathe,
or will at least be how
I try to whistle, when
the spirit moves.[4]

Deer-mice Singing Up Parnassus

for Bill and Lois Winchester

Sally Carrighar, in a meadow one night, heard what seemed a bird trilling, then saw it was a deer-mouse. My friend Bill Winchester tells me that when deer-mice came into his house from the tallgrass prairie of Oklahoma, he live-trapped and released them in a nearby hedgerow, but they waltzed back in, singing an epithalamium. Latin Musa, Greek Mousa, English Muse/Mouse linked by O—license to party on Parnassus and drink from Helicon. Sir Toby, Reepicheep, Sir Andrew & Feste grilling Malvolio about Pythagorean metempsychoses, can join them in a catch, a coranto, a galliard, jig, or sink-a-pace, singing to Moon and Stars, Diana and Venus. Blake's Sunflower seeks that sweet golden clime where the Traveler's journey is done—but Deer-Mice got there before tourists with FOX2P genes arrived (see *NY Times* 29 May 2009, p. A5: human "language gene" put into mice deepens their baby-cries).

In this "new" world they sing
as we come
down from
the stars,[1]
like Milton's Leonora singing
(aut Deus, aut vacui certè mens tertia
cøeli),[2]

they climb up the stems
of sunflowers still not weary
of

time,
and
they
trill,
perching and swinging,
in meadow and glade, as if
a rainbow
trout might rise
to
May-flies
from
their
music, as if John Muir and
Hetch Hetchy

might

come
back
alive and listening,
anadromous as
salmon or
sabretooth
tigers, up time itself into the glistening
moonlit
sonatas
of

Sierra
song.

Lara Mann

In the Absence of Bone Pickers

In the old days
when a Choctaw died
he was put on a scaffold
for months
until the flesh
came off easily.
The birds would
do their part and
the Bone Pickers the rest.
The bones were collected,
buried, making
the Mississippian Mounds.

Grandpa
a quarter Choctaw
called from Oklahoma
asked how I was doing
"up at that Yankee school"
said they had to put Duke,
my horse, down
because he was so foundered
he couldn't stand anymore.
Grandpa carried grain to him
for three months
and water
for a week
in the cattle pasture
on the original allotment.
He died there.
But because it was July
no rain for months
they couldn't dig a hole.

They dragged Duke
to the other pasture
on Aunt Annie's land
put him in a grove of trees
let the coyotes do their part.

Months later
when it rained
they dug his hole
had a marker made
engraved in steel
Duke: A Good Welsh Pony.
They found his bones,
mane, tail, hooves,
brought him home
to the original 160
"like the old Choctaws"
Grandpa said.
He didn't know
the ceremonial song
so instead he sang
Swing Low
Sweet Chariot
Coming for to carry me home.

Phil Young

Wetumka Is a Mythic Place

Wetumka is a mythic place, sacred ground
giving birth to more than thirteen or fifteen or sixteen family stories
of Greasy Creek and Carson stores,
cotton hoeing and Jesus coming
out of the East instead of the West,
of Possum belly cooked tender with new potatoes, carrots and small
    onions
thrown out to the dogs when its eating of "dead things" was questioned at
    table,
wild panthers breaking through screen doors on sultry summer nights,
    terrorizing
brothers who bravely hunted coon at night and stayed still when they
    heard and saw the child stomp dancing around Old Lady Little's place
    built on top of a Creek graveyard.
Of rugs pulled back and Victrola's cranked up
for dancin' the night away on polished hardwood floors,
under kerosene hurricane lamps lit high as daylight
cause the electric wired house with fancy push in pull out
switches wasn't turned on
for sharecroppers with thirteen kids.
Of striped candy sticks pulled from a toe sack with flour and sugar and
    coffee and salt,
Cloth almost ready for a shirt or skirt or sweat bandana
For fields on the share.

Wetumka is a mythic place, sacred ground
Of kinship with the post oak, persimmon and poke
picked from the fertile log whose retting gives it root,
too stubborn to be domesticated in fertilized, plowed rows or
lie in crowded beds of three or four covered with quilted squares of cherry
    tomatoes, Tennessee green beans,
insect resistant, malathion sprayed bells and okra pods,
Too much of a honky-tonk kind of green to ever become classical,

Too much Milk Cow blues to turn into Kaliga.
It always could answer yes or no, but on its own terms
At its own time of the year.
Good medicine root cut with cheap whiskey for whatever ails you.
Beware of ingesting it at the wrong time or it'll kill you.
It'll only be eaten with scrambled eggs and pepper sauce
Once a year within a few weeks. It's a mythic kind of green.

Wetumka II

Cousins by the millions and uncles and aunts
Would gather for reunions in Wetumka in my Grandpa and Grandma's
small wooden framed house, first one they had owned since coming to
Indian Territory in 1904.

They were sharecroppers, working someone else's land.
I still hear stories of "Old Lady Little's place" and other famous spots just
outside town,
Where life made its way out for them and their thirteen kids.

Most of my relatives lived in or near Wetumka (Wewoka, Seminole,
Calvin, Eufaula, Greasy Creek).
We used to find anything we could to put our plate on, from ironing
boards on the inside to upside down washtubs on the outside.
The tastes and smells sprinkled and mixed among the knick-knacks,
funeral calendars, and Folgers can anticipating the next delivery of brown
mule.
Chicken and dumplins, poke and potatoes
covered with gravy thick enough you could use it for wallpaper paste,
seasoned with enough grease, salt and pepper to keep you going for the
rest of the day.

Eggs weren't cooked good enough unless you could slide them easily
across your plate from the cast iron skillets of my Grandma Young.
The very best breakfast was fried eggs, fatback, bacon or sausage, all put
on the plate and biscuits broken in mouth sized pieces, drenched in that
gravy speckled with flecks of the meat of the morning.

When the hub of the wheel broke, we scattered like fireflies trying to find
their way home in the dark.
We still keep in touch, some still in Oklahoma, some still in California,
and me here in upstate New York.

I still remember our convincing Grandpa to get up and do
another jig dance across their flowered vinyl living room rug.
He would rise up and pull up his big baggy pants that were held
up by wide suspenders way above his belly button, and kick up
a lick like he used to do when he was a little boy dancing on the
tables in saloons in Arkansas, accompanied by the banjo playing
of his uncle.

Grandma would predictably yell, "Oh Will, cut out that foolishness." But
the grandkids would prevail and he would begin to dance. Like Mister Bo
Jangles, except that no one ever heard of Mr. Jangles. The only famous jig
dancer we knew was Grandpa, who always landed first on our hit parade.

The red clay that I often say still runs in my veins, was first seen by
me when I broke out in Henryetta. Even now, I slow down when I take
the turnoff the Beeline on my way to Wetumka. I pass through wondering
what it is like in this place where I was born.

Lise Erdrich

Y

"You shouldn't think so much," said her boyfriend. "It does something to your face." Y made no reply except to rearrange herself accordingly with a suitably dopey sexy smirk, glancing at the window of the downtown record store which reflected this: they looked like two 1970s rock stars, which was all she should aspire to. Smoke dope/drink wine/make love with him, Oh Wow. An older man of nineteen who initiated her into all these new non-ideas. If only she'd known. Y was always seeing thoughts all over the place, no matter where she looked or looked away from them, they'd be there. Gosh, he knew all the right people, had all the good stuff. A rich boy. He secretly would love her. "You fox," he said never guessing just how sly and clever. Y put her hands in the pockets of her jeans slouching carefully as if she were thinking about nothing like your little-cute-sweetpink-bubblegum-centerfold-partygirl was supposed to do, constructing herself in a more and more luscious dumb appealing pose than that. Sometimes a thought would come along and scare her clean out of her mind. It would chase her up and down the streets of small towns and big cities and even into the scenery: a jungle of revenge. Later on, she would chase the very same thought down and have her way with it whether or not it wanted to, and after that devour it. Oh and play with and toy with it too. Her boyfriend had been "found dead of an apparent overdose." (He never knew the line he crossed, a narcissistic injury that turned her heart to ice.) Y met many men and even some women in twenty years who liked that sort of game, who one by one went missing. And even, and especially her face with its ferocious inquisition, they were all seduced by and strangely neuronically attracted to the calm, quick, yellow eyes of a predator but nobody ever really knew Y.

ZANIMOO

Since you ask, what I was doing was fleeing, even before it happened I
mean, what I craved was to flee down every road up every rise in every
neck of the woods, the keen inclination and decline. How I loved the sweet
curves 90 per, the centrifugal force. The moon riding my shoulder on
the gleam of a lake and the soft black nightness swallowing, swallowing
the urge I'd become. Her long black hair loosening around me I thought.
Arrest me? I'm a caucasian, librarian, what did you say. I could flee all
night long as if consumed, not consuming, in the pursuit and avoidance
of my initial, chronic, acute, and terminal love. It drove me far beyond
alleged checkpoints of existentialist reality, flouting all boundaries,
groping the ghosty white trees and their superstitious depths with my
lights. Irrational aboriginal beliefs, nothing there for all your dark rumors
and inscrutable dread. Only a deer I'd flush out, an owl. God when he
spoke to me never mentioned his plan though I always felt satisfied with
the explanation that the crown of creation was Man. The spirits of animals
never troubled me when I lay down in my bed in the government quarters
to dream. It was that girl, how she leaped away, running, elusive as wind.
Even asleep, I could never get her to touch me. Instead the hideous
fact of my loneness compelled me. At first I could go to work then, not
dreaming, until the day I could never wake up. I was performing some
evident function but even as I spoke to visiting scholars with the help of
visual aids I perceived that something had followed. Thus it was I began
my long wrestle. Softer than cobwebs it was, and enveloping, causing me
to somehow adhere to beliefs. That waking was the wayward delusion
and error, that the thing at least would not itch. More silky I would say,
seductive, like satin sheets to lovers perhaps. My foe had no form or
substance and was remarkably resistant to even chance sudden words of
description. Sleep. I chose to call it sleep. Every blaze of sunrise I hurtled
into was victory, a glorious burst of sanguinary light. Just before the tenth
grade left her doe eyes had come out of a book and unzipped me. So of
course I had to try in different ways to contain the thing, hoping that no
one would notice. I had already given numerous other things up for Lent.
Yet could not bring myself to Confession, save for rubbing against some
girls between the bookshelves while reaching to fetch them their tomes.
Therefore, on this particular evening I feared to hear His voice in the
radio static or under the soda-pop-top, and listened the harder to local

Indians on their old-time memory show. Admittedly I was guzzling down
the road, peering at their tribal houses and romantic lives. Somewhere,
somewhere, in some yard I might see her, jumping a rope or whirling
beneath the swift spiral rush of her hair. Her dizzying feet placed just so
as she swung her small sister or brother, the fringe of her jacket, her skirt.
The yellow squares winked on as they gathered for supper, the blue glow
of TV, and then one by one winked back out. The peepshow was over,
the darkness unfurled. The deep psychological night then took place.
Meanwhile, two old women warbled in their lingo to apparent dismay, a
rising melodious river. When their words flowed back into English they
warned the public not to dance or to drink or to swear, to atone for all
sins and pray the Rosary and make the Easter Duty. Ah Maywee, don't
run about at night for the Rugaroo will surely catch up with you, they
concurred. It would be like a great black dog with burning red eyes, and
no one could hope to outrun it. Yet the old man who went out to play
cards way past midnight was here to tell the tale. Years ago, he claimed,
it had run alongside his wagon, silently pacing his horses. The words as
usual flowed back into French-Indian midstream, before I could grasp the
ending. In any case I keep this big gun beside me to resolve ambiguous
upshots. And my headlights were the only glowing eyes in the woods,
sweeping once more through the tall bony tress with their superstitious
depths. No. I did not. Mention. Suspicious deaths. For a time new memory
traces failed to form or you may call it a blackout. Then the sky was aglow
through the bare white branches, turning the dirty snow pink with purple-
blue shadows and the heart of lightness ascended. Racing again toward
daybreak, joyous salvation, I glanced very quick to the side. Only a scrap
of trash blown up by the wind, a plastic grocery bag or newspaper. These
roadside woods well rid of wild creatures and catching the comforting
detritus. I had read of the large carnivores and herds once numerous
here, grisly bears and dire howling wolves and vicious bloodthirsty
wolverines, skulking lions and lynx and unconverted Indians. Moose and
elk and bison and all the furbearing beavers. Also I keep this dictionary
to translate their odd words as they occur and transform: l'animal, plural,
lee zanimoo. The road snaked out before me with dull scraps of movement
creeping along the periphery. My eyes were on the red heart of fire in the
east that I strove for, scorning the trifling rubbish. A deep ecological sight
then took place.

Weather-beaten cardboard, loping persistently in the side view, distracted me to attention. It reared up in a sudden threatening attitude the size of a bear or refrigerator. They were chasing me, I realized with freak seismic tremors. In the rearview mirror a vengeful herd of debris took up the road, to the sides they leaped at the vehicle, everywhere the maddened scraps took form with the wind and multiplied, their growth only accelerating when I stepped on the gas. Zanimooooooooooooooozanimoooooooo they all howled as one, it came freezing through the cracks of my vehicle and seized me. 2,4, 5-polymerizedneoprenepolyisobutylepantherines, oooooooooooooooominous-bouncing polybutadinestyrenecopolymer puffrabbit, 2,4,D-fiendish-playful-rolypoly-terepthalicesterployamide-otters, horrible polyethylene wolverine, no end of indestructible plastic and elastomer creation. A Wonder Bread bag writhed from the snirt in the shape of a weasel, some paper-sack raptor, and eagle or hawk, swooped to swerve me. The faster I went the more bits I passed and each bit that I passed raised up from the ditch or a snag of the brush and joined the conglomerate intention. Pinkmink of fiberglass housefur, the huge beasts of rust—numerous compounds blew out of the earth just as winged polyvinylpredators plunged from the sky dropping garbage. Beer cans and liquor bottles smashed through my windows, you yourself call them evidence. They were all over me running and flying and crawling and then a large and strigiform tabloid—it resembled an owl with the glittering false eyes and breasts of an aging celebrity—plummeted garishly into my windshield, obliterating my vision and forcing me out of control. There was a brief inexplicable glimpse of biocide drums. I suppose then I slid finally into the void, but the officers recovered me, and that is all in the matter I recall.

Item, POLICE REPORT:
White man found in landfill, DWI. Turned over to county authorities and questioned in recent killings of yard dogs, prowling. Name withheld pending the additional charges.
Mekinaak Miniss Tribal News

Sara Marie Ortiz

Cord

Let the frame of things disjoint . . .

The cord of memory is this.

Aorta; capillaries,
silky wet red-black membrane
of the eye socket
without its eye.

Little terrible beautiful miracle of this: a temporal partial loss of my
peripheral vision. I was warned repeatedly by books, by doctors, by other
mothers, and all those who knew, about the drugs that'd be administered
before giving birth, warned about the long needles, the likelihood of this
or that, the way the drugs themselves would not take the pain away, no
not take it away at all, only change it, thus changing the birth itself and
its processes, thus altering even the light (or lack thereof) in the birthing
room. Every lens is altered. Thus I did not, could not, see the child body,
my child body, bringing her little life, little eyes (a cloudy dark watery
blue), little hands, little heart, into the world as they actually were. But,
I think this now, that in the way all things are altered, pain, lenses, light,
little heart, someway, this too—all flux as it lives for us and through us—
is good and beautiful.

She and I, we came alive to the world that day, and we still are.
Marrow, marrow, and marrow.
So much turns on light, or lack of light.
So much turns on the presence of light, or its marked absence.
Such light: *who can know it?*

Sing You Back

Chip Livingston

Crow Blue–Crow Black

(ink-voiced)

Crow Blue–Crow Black, I have come
to pacify you.

(paper-voiced)

Ha! Now your body is heavy.

(ink-voiced)

I have made your image out of black wood.

(paper-voiced)

*Now you are in a condition to follow
the red spider's path in all seven directions.
Ha! I have just come to fill you up.*

(ink-voiced)

Now, crow, with your back turned,
you are ligneous and black.

(paper-voiced)

*Forgetful
of my name and my people. Ha!
Now your heart is a dark thicket.*

(ink-voiced)

I have returned from the stars.
I have returned from the ground.

(paper-voiced)

*I do not need to say Blue.
I do not need to say U:ya.*

Punta del Este Pantoum

Accept my need and let me call you brother,
Slate blue oyster, wet sand crustacean,
In your hurrying to burrow, wait. Hover.
Parse opening's disaster to creation's

Slate, to another blue-eyed monstrous sand crustacean,
Water-bearer. Hear the ocean behind me,
Pursued, asking to be opened, asking Creation
To heed the tides that uncover you nightly.

Water-bearer, wear the water beside me,
Hide your burying shadow from the shorebirds,
But heed the tides that uncover you nightly.
Gems in sandcastles, stick-written words,

Hidden from the shadows of shorebirds,
Washed over by water. Water's revelatory
Gems, sand, castles, sticks, words—
Assured of erasure, voluntary erosion.

Watched over with warrior resolution,
Crab armor, claws, and nautilus heart,
Assured of a savior, reconstruct your evolution,
Clamor to hear, water scarab, what the tampered heart hears.

A scarab's armor is light enough to fly.
In your hurry to burrow, wait. Hover.
Hear the clamor of the crustacean's heart.
Heed this call of creation. Call me brother.

Septipus

for the seven-armed Uruguayo

1. One to hold the *mate;* to stop a taxi; to extend an index finger to push up loose-eared eyeglasses;

2. One to crook the thermos, pour the water, and redirect cooked *yerba* with a silver *bombilla;* to light a cigarette;

3. One to puff the *Rojo;* to gesture "*WWWHat a pity!!*"; to act out words our tongues don't know yet;

4. One to fine tune antennae and radiate little summer shocks; to tune the radio to María Rita, *tango electronica,* or The Cranberries;

5. One to good-guard new *amigos* from uneven stones and *otras cosas peligrosas,* bothers and malaria; to offer the growing moon, fireworks;

6. One to scribble a waitress a phone number; to correct a stress from an Italian accent;

7. One of rare perspective to photograph, spell out poetry, convert incantations, cast ordinary objects *artesanal.*

Together these brown arms shoulder the *mochila,* sign shipping orders, protect candles, smudge a room with incense; they envelop children in *abrazos.*

Embrace me also in these seven alchemical arms. Make the *tambores* jealous. Take my hand as we walk along the *rambla* becoming a new metal.

How Is It

we stopped for directions to Cabo Polonio
and I smelled *Fry bread?* It couldn't be,
I said, telling you quickly my hungry Indian
history. You replied *Estas son tortas fritas,*
una comida del campo desde hace mucho tiempo,
then *Oh my God, those are my grandfathers!*
And there they were, from Aguas Dulces,
visiting an old friend who ran the roadside stand,
a woman already wrapping the sweet dough
and packing it in a plastic bag with napkins
for us to eat on the sand dunes, trying to figure out
with your grandmother how long it had been
since the last time she'd seen you, only then
as tall as the hand she held at the pocket
of her thin denim skirt, and how was it again
that you and she were related. I watched this
in English, waiting to taste the difference
I wouldn't find in what your ancestors
and my ancestors fed us. How is it
we shared this flour and fat they fried
as golden as buttered toast, on a dune buggy
ride to a village without roads or electricity,
ate this ancient bread on ancient rocks
watching seals you call *los lobos*
de mar, envisioning a new Picasso?
We ate these *tortas* as the sun dove,
as the moon rose a day before it would be full,
telling each other the names of our appetites
in two languages winnowed down to basics:
Do you like me? Do you like the bread? How is it?

Jules Koostachin

Winter of Black Wiyas

Intolerable long and cold winter months,
Large white snowflakes falling from the cloudy grey skies above,

Cocoom, my grandmother prepares dark red raw *niska,* plucking and
    revealing the soul,
She hums to herself while working,

More than enough *wiyas* to keep winter bellies full and satisfied,
Frozen packed and stored in the outside shed, protected from the
    predators,

Mushoom, my grandfather, cleans his guns and old tools in the frosted back
    room,
Methodically organizing for his next hunting trip up north to the deepness
    of the bush,

Urban Inniuwak-awaskishuck stacking cards on the bare plywood chipped
    floor,
Hysterically laughing and rolling about, and crying with a shared pain of
    slivers,

Supper Time! *Mit-chi-su.* Come and eat!

Outside, *Windigo* wildly beats against the plastic covered windows,
Spirits scream to get inside from the cold darkness and smelling the food
    cooking,

Chilled breeze creeping in and my *apisis* white hands freeze,
Old wood stove is fed continuously with wood and smoke fills the shack,

Cocoom brings out the black meat, bannock and dumplings,
Geese was not my favorite,

Mushoom sits anxiously with an anticipating grumbling stomach and rubs
    his brown leathery strong hands together,

Frustrated at me when I refuse to *mit-chi-su,*
Hand reaching for candy, throwing it on top of my plate,

Once again reject eating the rich dark *wiyas,*
He laughs at me and shakes his head, asking himself where I came from

Black meat, so hard with a strong lingering smell,

My brothers show me up eating everything in front of them,
Eating the black meat, shot down from the northern sky,

Mushoom, the proud provider, hunting and trapping self sacrificed animals,
Cocoom smiles giving thanks to the generous spirits for feeding her family,

"Let's eat the black meat"—"Mit-chi-su" my quiet *Cocoom* says to us
    under her breath

Judi Armbruster

Living Rain

I lay in bed
Listening to the rain retreat.
So loud it had begun,
Pounding on our roof of tin
All hard staccato and gushing from the eaves.
Then it just leaves.
Slipping though the trees
Fading into the distance
Quiet once again.
Then I dreamt
Of Rain, a living being
With a breath that came and went.
I am rocked
Immersed in this moment of knowing.

Roberta Cordero

Bow-Riders

Standing in the bow with our rattles and clappers
we are singing up the dolphins:
our people made of ocean, born of rainbow.

There! a flipper!!
WHOOSH—they are with us!
peering up in greeting
jostling for the core of the bow wave
rocketing back in reprise

like us, a whole village on the move
this ocean everything they know
all they could need
or want
or imagine—
for 'alol'koy, there is no other home.

They vanish at hyper-speed
but for a mother and baby swimming in breathtaking synchrony
my sister looks me in the eye and I say,
Yes! I promise!
I will work to protect your baby's habitat!

There is no other home.

Tenille Campbell

Vancouver Airport, Gate B20
December 6th, 2008—6:04 am

I'm coming home leaving home finding home
a coffee shop mocha scalds my tongue
an egg mimosa soothes my stomach
the glow of the laptop flickers shadows across my face
where am I going? what am I doing?
something's different

home is in the far north in the Saskatchewan bush
a regulated two story reserve house cresting the banks
of a valley that echoes throughout our first nation
home in is my mother's arms skinny and lean and freckled
in my mother's face wrinkled and thinning hair and wide glasses
home is in my father's smile as he welcomes me
his kisses on my cheek as I throw my head back and laugh

yet I am leaving home leaving my safe place leaving you
in the drizzling rain before dawn
outside the glaring lights in front of canadian departures
we kissed softly you tasted of toothpaste you smelled of sleep
missing you missing home missing us

I sit here typing in the anonymous of airports
stomach full coffee empty laptop flickering
between home and home

Joseph Bruchac

Steel

for Rick Hill and in memory of Buster Mitchell

I

Steel arches up
past the customs sheds,
the bridge to a place
named Canada,
thrust into Mohawk land.

A dull rainbow
arcing over
the new school,
designed to fan
out like the tail
of the drumming Partridge—
dark feathers of the old way's pride
mixed in with blessed Kateri's
pale dreams of sacred water.

II

When that first span
fell in 1907
cantilevered shapes collapsed,
gave like an old man's
arthritic back.

The tide was out,
the injured lay trapped like game in a deadfall
all through that day
until the evening.
Then, as tide came in,
the priest crawled
through the wreckage,
giving last rites
to the drowning.

III

Loading on,
the cable lifts.
Girders swing
and sing in sun.
Tacked to the sky,
reflecting wind,
long knife-blade mirrors
they fall like jackstraws
when they hit the top
of the big boom's run.

The cable looped,
the buzzer man
pushes a button
red as sunset.
The mosquito whine
of the motor whirrs
bare bones up to
the men who stand
an edge defined
on either side
by a long way down.

IV

Those who hold papers
claim to have ownership
of buildings and land.
They do not see the hands
which placed each rivet.
They do not hear the feet
walking each hidden beam.
They do not hear the whisper
of strong clan names.
They do not see the faces
of men who remain
unseen as those girders
which strengthen and shape.

Prints

Seeing photos
of ancestors
a century past

is like looking
at your own
fingerprints—

circles
and lines
you can't
recognize

until someone else
with a stranger's eyes
looks close and says
that's you.

The Turn

My mother's father kept his general store
for forty years on the corner where
Middle Grove and the wide State Road
intersect at Splinterville Hill.

There the hooves of long-vanished horses
coming up the road splintered the planks
which paved the highways way back then.
Teams strained up the hill, then made
the turn to Glass Factory Mountain
where bottles were blown to hold Saratoga's
healing waters, that flowing gift
of Rawenio, the one whose breath
holds up the heavens.

Long before I was born, my grandfather kept
two tubs out by the watering trough.
There children brought him turtles and toads
saved from the dangers of new roads
cut through hills where foot trails woven
by our old people circled this sacred land.

Each spring, when shadows washed over the hill,
Grampa Jesse would close the store for the night,
turn off the lights and, in that quiet dark,
return the turtles back to the brook,
place the toads in his garden or out in the woods.

Late last night, driving a winding road,
a spring rain washing my vision,
I stopped to pick up from the blacktop a toad.
Holding it in one hand, I drove with the other,
as it throbbed a throat-full double note
an echo of my own heart's rhythm.

It sang to me my grandfather's song,
all the way up to Splinterville Hill
to the place where we turned together.

Allison Adelle Hedge Coke

Platte Mares

Migratory Sandhill Cranes rise into spiraled kettles, their
mares purring chortling kettling vortex siege sedge herd.
Vortexing themselves into dawn, dusk.

Call & response.
Call & response. Call & response. Call & response.

Tens of thousands looping high over mustang running buffalo sod.
Mares above, below.
Last year's colts breaking out into adolescent gangs,
adolescent gangs, colt crane cohorts,
bachelor flock.
Over colt mustangs turning.
The mares above turning yaw.

My filly snapping teeth on cool air.
Her lead mare calling, she neighs quick.
Sandhills display, spread wings, preen, arch, calling, fluff out
toward intruders cranes/coyotes.

All mares facing off the canine bite.
Territory three to two-fifty acres.
Nares, mandible.
Unison call, antiphonal territorial call, mated postures vocalized.

Covert lining flight feathers, primaries along the wing hand, propulse
forward,   secondaries, forearm inside primaries, soar and stop,
tertials of upper arm,
bustling close to the body—
estrous cycle cloaca oviduct—
Preparing for two egg clutch,
egg tooth tubercle horn. Precocial pipping breath,
hock tarsus—The ground mares fetlock proofed as well.

Kettling, converging, calling—home.
It is the season.

Linda Hogan

First Language

The water here is different every moment.
It is a place of everything changing,
even the sounds.
Some call them changers of language
tellers of stories.
I say they were here the first day of sky creation
when one of our many gods said or thought,
let there be infinite sky
and creatures with wings,
a red setting sun of feathers
over the golden eye
as if to disguise what is seen,
all of them now looking dark,
as if they believe they are hidden,
settled together for the night
where they will be
tall ones standing
noisy and singing,
talking,
new ones arriving from the four directions,
from the horizon
as if up from the ground
instead of from the sky,
the long neck of the planet
crying out, ancient beginnings.
Here they come. Listen.
Coming near to us.

Here they come, gathering,
standing close to us,
speaking out to us
all together,
island of crane,
all one mind,
altogether
speaking
our first language.

The Sandhills

The language of cranes
we once were told
is the wind. The wind
is their method,
their current, the translated story
of life they write across the sky.
Millions of years
they have blown here
on ancestral longing,
their wings of wide arrival,
necks long, legs stretched out
above strands of earth
where they arrive
with the shine of water,
stories, interminable
language of exchanges
descended from the sky
and then they stand,
earth made only of crane
from bank to bank of the river
as far as you can see
the ancient story made new.

Kim Blaeser

A crane language.

From where behind you ancient light enters. A fissure
in the propriety of reason. No trailing words or sound. Only first
translucence. Sun turning the hose of your throat to a vessel
of fire. Arthurian sword of your tongue, angled like a
sundial against the cup of all reluctance. Stone. Or flesh.
This torch of language held in the weighted anchor of time.

Still the flame of your tongue gives light.

Some Kind of Likeness

Again today it happened. At my feet I saw the grey bird wing, just one
severed from the bird. Slight and curved in the remembered form.
With my backward glance the texture unmasks itself, becomes a small
fallen segment from a tree. The weathered wood surfaces from
feathers. I stand before them—wing, wood, wing, wood, wing—back
and forth. The grey shape drawn, erased, redrawn, hovering like bird
or bark on the edge of realities. Holding the air-thin space between
sight and vision.

Song of the Frail Branch

> from Victor Hugo: Be as a bird perched on a frail branch that
> she feels bending beneath her, still she sings away all the same,
> knowing she has wings.

I

Indigo bunting. Merganser. Fork-tailed flycatcher. Yellow-bellied
sapsucker. Tufted titmouse. Names that fly off your tongue. Paint the
palette of your imagination. Rufous-sided towhee. Scarlet tanager.
Eyebrowed thrush. Umbrella bird. White-faced storm petrel. Chimney
swift. Black-capped gnatcatcher. Flocks and fledglings. Poults. Broods.
Covey. Gaggle of geese. Murder of crows. Parliament of owls. Charm of
finches. A bounteous bevy of bird words.

II

Common red-breasted robins devour fourteen feet of earthworms
each day. Tubular-tongued hummingbirds stream by at fifty-miles-an-
hour. These iridescent aerial artists flying backwards and upside down.
Macaw beaks wield bite strength of seven hundred pounds per square
inch. Just enough to break the weld on metal cage bars. Backyard pigeons
regurgitate crop milk for their young. And ornithologists record elaborate
bird rituals. The maligned magpies laying wreaths of grass near their dead.
Birds billing, clasping and holding the beaks of mates in courtship. But
who could believe the myth of flight?

III

Sweet hollow home woven of moments. Collected strands of feathered
flight. Warp and weft of territory. Spherical courtship nests lashed into
cattails. Soft swaying oriole pouch. Jay's shaggy shanty cast in the crotch of
a tree. Bowl. Hid-e-hole. Mud-lined adobe. Roost. Burrow. Bird bungalow.
Teacup to bathtub sized. Grass, weeds, fur, and hair. Feathers, bark, and
dung. Forming treetop havens for hatching. Knot-hole nests and grass
dome huts. Our everyday forests filled each season with airy dwellings
built of fairytale props: lichen and spiderwebs, thistledown and caterpillar
silk. Bird shelter–human sanctuary.

IV

Speckled ovals, tumbled from elfin imagination. Incubate. Clutch. Of eggs. Robin blue. Olive. Mottled brown. The parasitic cuckoo who colors her eggs to match those of her host. Literary oology. Collecting. Candling. Pea-sized hummingbird. And the ostrich egg, four thousand seven hundred times larger. The wonder of shell and membrane. Domesticity of yolk and embryo. Imagine the fragile, china-thin sphere beneath the weight of hen. Then witness the pip and crack by egg tooth. Fault-line opening to emit awkward orange-legged offspring. Hatch. Hatchling. Brood.

V

Thimble-full of pink nakedness. Rope throats stretching, beaks lifting, passel of tiny heads nudge, stack and unstack, positioning the virgin, fathomless hunger of their mouths before the bounty of the mother's beak. Monstrous membrane of eyes bulging for earth sight.

VI

Delicate trilling tongues. Song box throats. Peeps, tweets, caws, and chirps. Mourning dove's *coo-ah coo coo*. The lost-child wail of the catbird. Winnowing wings of the snipe. Whistling duck. *Whip-poor-will.* Cardinal calling the question *whoit whoit whoit?* Persistent *peck peck peck* of the pileated foraging for food. Quack, caw, honk, and *hoo hoo hoot*. Lilting dawn operas, nightingale's evensong, and northern lake's lonesome loon lullaby. Symphonic sound of birds naming themselves over and over in song–*chick-a-dee-dee-dee-dee*.

VII

The inflated red pouch of the frigate bird. Elaborate head-throw of the winter goldeneye. White cheek-patch flashing against river water. Spring woods and the steady insistent thrumming of the partridge. Northern harrier turning midair cartwheels. Long black-tipped wings climbing skyward, ever skyward, then turning, now dropping. A streaking raptor. Sinking, diving, grey-hooded skywriter. Feathered dancers. Drumming. Ritualized displays. Peacocks strutting like Vegas show girls. Males seeking mates. Vavavavoom. Birds gone wild.

VIII

Airy and aerodynamic. Lithe and lifting. Language falters at feathers.
Tender tufts of snowy down. Cinnamon sprinkles on porridge gray.
Wisps and strokes of ivory insulation touched with teardrop notes of
color. Buff. Caramel. Rufous-brown. Artistry accumulated in layers, in
the tints and hues of intention, the blush of beauty and extravagance.
Hollow spirit fibers. Quills dressed for courtship or camouflage. Canary
yellow. Cardinal red. Sooty black. Cobalt or iris blue. Brazen busts of flight
feathers, inked with fine lines like Japanese scrolls. The rudder and balance
of tail. Patterned plumage sheltering peacock eye. Bands, bars, stripes,
and blissfully random swatches and patches of variegated vestments. Swift
sleek filters. Fashioned of light. Flight. The ultimate allure of air.

IX

Huma, fire bird of Sufi fable. Perhaps legless he flies and never rests.
Perhaps like the phoenix he burns and rises. Trickster Raven of Puget
Sound. Wandering over this god-earth he stumbles into truth. Cosmic egg
of Estonia—is it you that births our world? All these fruitful flights of bird
legends and mythic fancy. Stories and dream songs we hatch and warm
beneath the metabolic fire of human longing. Our incubation patches,
perhaps an ancient hunger for faith.

X

Be as a bird perched on a frail branch. Aerofoils tucked against fine-
boned body. Thousands upon thousands of feathers at the ready. Grasping
evolution in the four-toed flexed arc of its claw. And when we feel earth
bending beneath our human soles. We stand. Still. Watching you. Flex
and lift. Warbling again toward white, knowing by flight, where winter sky
tangles with glory.

Karenne Wood

Deer Woman

He hunted me into the clouds as I sought the blue
star-petaled flower, its scent like magnolia and pears.
I left my family in the meadow to pick my steps
across patched snow, where fields grasped edges of the sky.

There is within some of us a longing to be stripped clean.

Alongside, the forest held his shape. His scent rose to me
with the wind. Too late I knew him, too late to find cover,
and I ran as I was made–haunches taut, nostrils steaming,
in flight like a swallow, I ran into glistening whiteness.

When I tired, he was there, his circle tightening by the hour—
dark, and dark-eyed, hypnotic—I could feel his hunger's fist
as my own. I had taunted his dreams more than once,
dreamt that mouth, the whole darkness of him.

There is within some of us a longing to be stripped clean,

to give it all—red strings of sinew, tufted hair, marrow,
white ropes of fat, to bare the body's pulse. I froze,
heavy with the need to dissolve into him, his mouth
the deep red song of an appeasable desire.

On the wind, I hear another song, my family calling out
to me, calling me into my name. But I cannot return
from this altitude, bound to his hunger, which is a kind
of love. I will kneel in a cloud's wisp of grace, to discover

how completely our own wanting wounds us.

To Keep Faith

It's an idea like light, the star's trajectory
over a sacred place that rises from its landscape:
dark butte, dark desert tower, dark river swelling
across the shadowed plains of the republic.

This is your passion: to save the earth's cathedrals.
The machinery of our country's interests works against it.
In another city, you might have disappeared,
blindfolded at sunrise with hands behind your back.

In another time, not long ago, I might have
found you face up in a field of silence among the still-
beautiful bodies of Dakota men. To speak
for the land: even our history is against us here.

But I have imagined loving you—the perfection of your skin,
its holiness—tongues like salmon coupling in the rush
of white rapids, flash of bodies entwined through
the waterfall's tumult, and wondered whether I would do it,

as though you hadn't already recalled who I was
before I learned to be wary of histories or as though
your words hadn't entered me like light,
small wavecaps riding on all that darkness.

For you, then, some words about light. Relentless,
earthly light. Incantatory words we could lick
like blue sparks. Words to keep faith with each other
and the earth's searing love, which still claims us.

Simon Ortiz

from *Spiral Lands/Chapter 3,* Simon J. Ortiz and Andrea Geyer

1.

I've been here before.

Something in the bone. Remembers. And the hands and arms.

Stone. Canyon. A sandstone bluff south of here where the canyon opens onto the desert plain.

And in the small wind I am conscious of as I top the ridge right below the sandstone shelf the little village is built upon. And I listen for anything. Wherever this place is.

It could be southern Colorado, some miles from the Four Corners. What is now called Four Corners.

It could be Utah also. Same place. Same place. That's what I think. But perhaps I am trying to tie myself personally to this. Same place.

A tie. A link. A connection. But I don't know. I'm indigenous to this region of the Southwest. Aacqu is south, quite a bit south, of that place.

Same place. Something in the bone. Remembers.

When I see the walls of the little village I remember. My ancestor must have thought the same as I have: I've been here before.

Scraggy and tough pinyon tree anchored into the stone. The jay chirp and screeee—ch. A thousand years ago perhaps. A thousand whiles that become part of the notion of forever.

Something in the bone remembers, always remembers.

2.

Horizon. Thin fir at the very top. Not far away. Horizons are always like that. Close. Standing on this ground or little road, we are the ground and the little road. We are the horizon.

When I was appointed Tribal Interpreter-Translator for the tribe by the Antelope elders, my cousin-brother Bobby showed me which brush thicket to approach so I could gather material for prayer sticks.

Hard, tough, finger-size branches. Duwah, Robert said, pointing. And he took some corn meal from the bag at his side. And I did the same, following him. Always, he said, you have to ask permission. And pray. Pray. Pray thanks. He began to murmur. And I did the same, following him.

Canyon sides are steep crumbling cliffs of sandstone. Fir standing straight up on the slanting canyon slopes. Yes, just like the canyon sides where the brush grew.

Wind and birds. And sun at mid-day. Shadows are close to stone. It hasn't rained for weeks. Or months. You can tell by the air. Be thankful anyway. Beyond the horizon to the west, the sky is empty. Blue dry sky. Shadows close to cliff stone.

Once as boys my brothers and I went for wood toward Sraa-kaiyaah.

Charley and Bill, our wagon-plow-general work horses. Up the winding road through canyon south of McCarty day school. My younger brothers—Gilly, we used to call him that until years later when he became Petuuche, and Earl, the youngest—and me. I was about fourteen years old.

Several miles northeast of Sraa-kaiyaah, suddenly the wagon wheel struck a big stone boulder, jerking the wagon tongue violently! Dammit! We could hear the crack! I immediately pulled back the reins and applied the hand brake.

We stopped. And I jumped off the wagon to check the tongue. It split toward the front and extending back toward the front of the wagon. Broken wagon tongue. A disaster.

Breathe deep. What are we gonna do? It happens, it happens. Boys. We.
Us. Feeling at a total loss. What to do, what to do? I looked around and
thought. And thought.

We had come to a halt by a stand of dry pinyon and juniper. That's where
we were. I looked around, and I knew where we were. There was a canyon
not far away where old man Bowtuwah had a sheep camp. I said to Gilly
and Earl, Go and get wire. If Bowtuwah is there, ask him for wire. Say we
need wire to fix a broken wagon tongue so we can drive home. Also find a
straight board to make a brace. In the meantime, I'll get wood and load the
wagon. And I pointed the direction where they were to go into the canyon.

Here in this canyon, there are firs; the elevation is higher. Horizon is still
the horizon. At home, the mesas above Deetseyaamah have juniper and
pinyon. It's dry just like here too. Horizon is the ground and the little road.
We are right there, a mile and half from where the canyon begins. And
where you follow a little road downward into the flat dry land below.

3.

It could be grass anywhere.
Dry as ever.
Thin as ever.
Year upon year.
Ever upon ever.

When you look at the land, and you breathe the hot breeze, you don't really
    think.
I mean you don't really think about the hot dry time you've lived in days
    past.
You simply accept them; you simply know the climate and weather is always
    that.
The days are yours; you, in a sense, don't mind because they are yours,
    always.
That time I tried to walk to Chaco, I took a bus to Grants, then caught a
    cab.
To a local hotel, near the Grants Cafe & Bar. It didn't matter where I was.

A Route 66 hotel where a million people had stayed before; you could feel
    them.
All over the place, in the cracked parking lot, on the doorstep, in the thin
    curtains.

Dreams go.
They go. Doesn't matter
Where.
Grass, grass, grass everywhere.
Even in a crummy town like Grants.
Piled, crushed, matted down
Against the poor corner made
By the cracked asphalt and the wall
Painted a dull yellow something or other.

Walking over to the Grants Cafe & Bar I felt nauseous suddenly, you know,
Like I'm going to throw up, like I'm going to lose it all on the front door
Of the cafe and bar before I even had a drink yet. What's wrong with you?
Yeah, I was talking to myself. Walking by myself and talking to and by
    myself.

When I did go through the door without barfing, a waitress looked at me
    closely
And didn't know what else to do except wave a menu at me and mumble
    "Lunch?"
No, I said, and looked at diners seated at tables against the walls, white
    people

Mostly, so I didn't say anything but shook my head. No. No. And walked
    past.

Into the bar.
Shadow.
Dreams go, like I said.
It doesn't matter where.
They just go.
Before you know it,
They're gone.

4.

All that distance
From here to there.
A sweeping view, I think you would call it.
Grass, yucca, sagebrush, in the far, far distance
Juniper, maybe some scrub pinyon.
So far away even the horizon is misty.
Kaweshtima, I think, seen from this side.
Once I started a long walk to Chaco Canyon.
Years and years. Ago now. A shaky memory.
Drinking too much then, years and years.
And trying to quit. Quit for months, even years.
Once or twice. It was like that for years.
All that distance from here. Now. To there.
Back then. A view sweeping to the past.
From here looking south. Somewhat east.
Shadows and dimension. Place and time.
I can't believe it sometimes, you know.
How we pass through, how we manage.
Yet we do. No matter what has happened.
Looking from here on this low knoll
You can see everything. Everything about time and place.
Everything about time. Everything about place.

Sherwin Bitsui

Flood Song

I walk my hair's length over tire ruts,
crush seed pods with thumbnails
push kernels of corn
into dove's nests on the gnarled branches of our drowned lungs.

Mining saguaro pulp from garden rock,
squeezing coarse black hair—
I arrive at a map of a face buried in spring snow.

With a plastic cup
I scrape the enamel chips of morning songs
    from the kitchen sink,
and breathe through my eyelids,
glimpsing the thawing of our flat world.

I dial into the blue skin of the map's stiff pulse,
emeralds spill from the skull's cavernous wail,
but nightfall is still darkest
in the middle stanza of the poem
    arching twenty miles past forgiveness.

The poem
held out to the wind
speaks *juniper* to the wilderness,
as August slithers into September's copper pipes
searching for the paw print of a waterfall
on the mind's lunar surface.

Here—I thread nightfall into the roan's black mane.
Here—I peel a paper mask from the hare's moist cartilage.
Here—tornadoes twist into the loom's black yarn,
but the premonition—
beginning with three masts and a cross—
still mushrooms over the groans of husbands and wives
folding their petals outward
from their salt-coated bodies
saying:
    nihi yazhi, nihaaneendza,
        nihi yazhi, nihaaneendza.

    our child, you have returned to us,
        our child you have returned to us.

I wanted to swallow the song's flowers, swim diagonally its
    arched back, its shadow stinging my hands with black pollen.

We were on the same surgical table waiting for the surgeons to
    carve us back into shape.

The drum pulsed somewhere in the dark and I heard a woman
    unbraiding her hair.

I felt morning songs leap from the *hooghan's* smoke-hole and
    curl outward from the roof of the sky, gliding through us like rain.

I sang, sang until the sun rose.

The shadows of my face grew into a swallow with folded wings
    and darted into the fire.

A cloud became a skull and crashed to the earth above Black Mesa.

The cloud wanted to slip through the coal mines and unleash its horses.

It wanted to crack open bulldozers and spray their yolk over the hills so
    that a new birth cry would awaken the people who had fallen asleep.

It wanted to push their asymmetrical ramblings into the weft of storm blanket,
    dye it hazel and sink it into the rising waters.

A city dragged its bridges behind it and finally collapsed in a
    supermarket asking for the first apple that was ever bitten.

No one questioned the sand anymore.

No one un-tucked themselves from their bodies and wandered
    the streets without knowing their clans.

Everyone planted corn in their bellies and became sunlight
    washing down plateaus with deer running out of them.

The phone was ringing through it all.

The line was busy when I picked the axe
    and chose the first tree   to chop down.

Allison Adelle Hedge Coke

America, I Sing You Back

> a tribute for Phil Young, my father Robert Hedge Coke,
> Whitman, and Hughes

America, I sing back. Sing back what sung you in.
Sing back the moment you cherished breath.
Sing you home into yourself and back to reason.

Oh, before America began to sing, I sung her to sleep,
held her cradleboard, wept her into day.
My song gave her creation, prepared her delivery,
held her severed cord beautifully beaded.

My song helped her stand, held her hand for first steps,
nourished her very being, fed her, placed her three sisters strong.
My song comforted her as she battled my reason
broke my long held footing sure, as any child might do.

Lo, as she pushed herself away, forced me to remove myself,
as I cried this country, my song grew roses in each tear's fall.

My blood-veined rivers, painted pipestone quarries
circled canyons, while she made herself maiden fine.

Oh, but here I am, here I am, here, I remain high on each and every peak,
carefully rumbling her great underbelly, prepared to pour forth singing—

and sing again I will, as I have always done.
Never silenced unless in the company of strangers, singing
the stoic face, polite repose, polite, while dancing deep inside, polite
Mother of her world. Sister of myself.

When my song sings aloud again. When I call her back to cradle.
Call her to peer into waters, to behold herself in dark and light,
day and night, call her to sing along, call her to mature, to envision—
Then, she will quake herself over. My song will make it so.

When she grows far past her self-considered purpose,
I will sing her back, sing her back. I will sing. Oh, I will—I do.

America, I sing back. Sing back what sung you in.

Lee Maracle

eyes wide open

I want to walk around the world with my eyes wide open
fearless in the looking
At its cold hard steel wired beauty, its soft underbelly of ugliness
Its smooth wrinkles
Its austere ostentation
Its innocent criminality
Its guilt-wracked wonderment
Its insane reasonability
Its odd repetition
Its strange familiarity
Its dead life.

I want to couple huckleberry blossoms with old worn out shoes
In some magical way that teaches the world the distance between Navvy
    jack's
smooth round stones and white eagles landing on the moon

I want to marry the smooth skin of square shouldered men
with the inelegance of a Swede saw slicing cedar at the roots.
in a way that promotes the dreaming pair of cultural promise

I want to see the world as crystal clean as swamp born mosquitoes
feeding frog, feeding swamp, feeding cattails and wild garlic
and finally watch those swamp drops move on up to sky to pour down as
    the
        sweetest rain

I'm home again

August 2, 2000—Hedgebrook

I'm home again.

Blue-hued dark green islands jut up to reach the sky
Still looking as though they are still struggling to become flatlands
valleys and lush green meadows
They didn't quite make it most of them
They remain cedar and fir decked
mountain edges of earth
tied to the deep

The sea holds these her baby lands,
bathing them in her white capped evening water
rocking them as though it were the ferry standing still
and the islands moving
Memory pulls at my skin,
images punch holes in this moment
of awe over the vista the not quite born islands make.
My body knows these islands

The story of this corridor belongs to Suquamish boatmen
ferrying families from one end of its territory
to the other. Cedar and ermine skin clad women ancestors
stand regal in the canoes while brown skinned men
Dip and sing through the slate under-bellied
Blue-green water.

Conquest silenced these boatmen
stilling the story of canoes for a time to waken in the first year
of my birth. This meander feels so familiar
I have to wonder whether or not I am impressed.

I'm home again.
This journey from Squamish, B.C. post-cultural prohibition
in 1951 to Hedgebrook in the summer of 2000,
38 years after our emancipation
is fraught with the urgent watery aloneness
only writers feel.

The aloneness of paddling about in our
various sociological and historical swamps,
weaving snippets of dream word we selected to play with
onto the loom of our imagination
harnessing language
to plough new soil,
create new story, is thick, omnipresent here.

I'm home again.
My pathway here is strewn with sharp stones
singing confusing songs of yearning.
My bones,
my personal stones,
sing back songs of yearning—
Tsuniquid's yearning.
I watch myself highstep my way to this language
This pen
This paper
this place.

The stones' razored edges bleed white as the faces of my dead
emerge, embossed by the shadows in the center of each stone.
Between the stones holding their faces, ribbons of light flicker
Snippets of my busyness shine inside each ribbon of light.
I watch myself steal moments to create art.
Coolly and deliberately I let go of Lucucid
Grieve the parking of my original language
And bury it inside my bones.

I pick up the volumes of books cradling the text of this language.
I feel the sand-papering this language once was and re-watch as my body
smoothes the rough edges as the words journey through me
See-yah becomes saskatoon,
si-siutl becomes sea serpent,
Tsuniquid becomes the mother of thought
Thought becomes hidden being,
Hidden being becomes a spiral down to a moment of peace and recognition
Knowing becomes a spiral out to meet the world.
This sea, this new Tsuniquid forms the structure of my being.

I'm home again.
Killer whales sidle their litheness alongside the ferry.
Cedar bows acknowledging my return
Raven calls out a cackled hello.
Berries look ready to greet me.
Even the sea peels back its tide
To permit a trek across her mud just as I land
I can see the wetlands from the hill near my cottage
The tears come.

I'm home momma.
Haitchka for leading me here
Haitchka my dead for fussing over language for me
Haitchka to those who came before me,
for story
For song,
for dance.
You paved my journey home with light and alacrity.

I am home again.
Suquamish voices are everywhere here.
I am so totally old and so completely new here.
I pull fragments from old file cabinets,
splinters of memory,
Bind them together to re-shape my world.
I weave this imagined dream world onto old
Squamish blankets,
history-hole-punched and worn—
to re-craft today,
to re-member future in this new language
And I sing I am home again.

Duane Niatum

Riding the Wake of the Paddle Journey

Laxaynam, our canoe, parts the water
the way waves pass through wind currents,
    curl back upon themselves.

This island passage is a body of voices
and salmon swimming beside us. We will
    hear the animal people and eagles

each winter ceremony and in the fathoms
of sleep. We glide over whitecaps as Sea Wolf
    chants and channels our blood

in the paddles' thrust. In the wake of our guardian
we return to this path to be servants of our ghosts,
    the family keeping the storytelling stone

that shows our flesh's formed by tide and stump.
The tide churns and weaves a braid opposite
    the direction taking us to tamahnous fires.

We offer the sea splashing our hands
and faces a cedar bough for the dead to transform
    their long ago grief that never leaves

the darkness on our tongues. Gulls hover above
the bow of Laxaynam; goose-bumps crawl down
    our skin; Old Ones peer at us from gull eyes.

Soon we will reach our Puyallup friends, build
a fire and make our bed on the sandbanks.
    We pull like ospreys and bears toward

First People's lodge, consistent as the breakers;
breathe salt and driftwood air between the sea
    and Takopid, mountain of white water streams

and lake whose shells speak the words of pipers
and coots far below who rise from surf and fall
    from the blue-green marsh-basket.

Drifting to the beach, we point our paddles toward
the white trail in the sky, honor Xaʔeʔf, the Changer,
    and the mountain keeping our heart

as broad and deep as the red elderberry sky.
We honor the hosts, the Puyallups, our family,
    children, and elders greeting us from shore;

their drum and song a sunlight flame circles
the birth of water stories, the smokehouse path
    of sun, wolf, and Thunderbird.

Notes

Jace DeCory, "Sam, I Am"

This was written with all my love and to let you know how much I respect and honor the way that you have chosen to live for us. You are the most courageous person I have known in my life, and I pray that our sons will continue living their lives in the same way—with love, faith, hope, and especially, courage. Thank you for sharing your life with me. Mitakuye Oyasin. Love, your wife, Jace (2/14/02)

Carter Revard, "Aesculapius Unbound"

1. In Ovid's *Metamorphoses,* Book 15 (lines 622–744), he tells how Apollo's son Æsculapius, god of healing, changed himself into the great serpent that twines about his staff, and in that form was brought by the Romans from the ancient Greek shrine in Epidaurus to Rome and installed, as the God of Healing, in a new shrine on an island in the Tiber, where he healed the Romans of a terrible plague. Earlier in Book 15, Ovid's spokesmen tell how the world was created and continually changes (humans are reincarnated, and some in previous lives were animals); they advocate a vegetarian diet instead of killing and eating sheep, goats, and oxen, and deplore animal sacrifices to the gods. Finally, Ovid ends this last book of his *Metamorphoses* by narrating recent and future Roman history: Julius Caesar's assassination and his transformation into a god (a star in heaven); the ascent to imperial power of Caesar's adopted son Augustus Caesar; and the future ascent to heaven of Augustus, who will "there, removed from our presence, listen to our prayers." In the last nine lines of the poem, Ovid prophesies that his poetry will also be immortal: "through all the ages shall I live in fame."

2. This at least is the Darwinian creation story, as told in encyclopedias under the entry for Reptiles. This story says birds and snakes evolved as branches of Reptilia, and that mammals bloomed on another branch of that tree, so we human (including the Oklahoma cowboy who shot the egg-stealing snakes, and the boy who witnessed that and heard an oriole sing) also hang, not far away, on this tree of life.

3. See George Economou, *Ananios of Kleitor* (Exeter, England: Shearsman Books, 2009), Fragment 18, "Melampous overheard the worms overhead" (p. 20), and the Endnote on this, pp. 88–89, for the story of Melampous, who received the gift of

hearing and understanding the speech of animals, and consequently the gift of prophecy, from some serpents, because he had ceremonially cremated the body of their mother, whom he had found "a sacrificial victim, beside an oak tree. In gratitude . . . these serpent children licked his ears as he slept, purifying him and enabling him to understand the language of birds and animals, which he used to foretell the future." Thanks, George: sometimes the gifts borne by Greeks are better than Trojans.

4. Acts of the Apostles 2.1–6:

1. And when the day of Pentecost was fully come, they were all with one accord in one place.

2. And suddenly there came a sound from heaven as of a rushing mighty wind, and it filled all the house where they were sitting.

3. And there appeared to them cloven tongues like as of fire, and it sat upon each of them.

4. And they were all filled with the Holy Ghost and began to speak with other tongues, as the Spirit gave them utterance.

. . .

6. every man heard them speak in his own language.

Carter Revard, "Deer-mice Singing Up Parnassus"

1. In our Osage naming ceremonies, it is said that we have come to this world from the stars. The words in one of our dawn-songs say of the Sun: "He returns, he is coming again into the visible world."

2. For Milton's epigram Ad Leonoram Romæ cantentem, of which this is line 5, see John Milton, *Complete Shorter Poems,* ed. Stella Revard (Wiley-Blackwell, 2009), p. 199, where a note explains: "This and the two epigrams following were composed either in late 1638 or early 1639 for the famous Neapolitan singer Leonora Baroni, whom Milton heard sing during one of his visits to Rome. She was later celebrated by Italian poets in a volume of commemorative poetry, *Applausi Poetici alle Glorie della Signora Leonora Baroni* (Rome, 1639)." The English translation (by L. Revard, on p. 199) is:

> A winged angel from heaven's ranks itself is made
>
> guard to each of us. Believe this, people.
>
> What wonder, Leonora, if your glory's greater,
>
> for your voice itself sounds God's presence.
>
> Surely God or an emptied heaven's third intelligence,
>
> hidden, empowering, glides through your throat,

empowering, glides and simply teaches mortal hearts

to grow accustomed to immortal sound.

For if God's all, and fused with all, then within you

he speaks as one and, silent, holds the rest.

For *mens tertia,* "third intelligence," the editor cites Ficino's *Commentary* on Plato's *Symposium* 2.4.

Richard Van Camp, "Calendar for the folks from my hometown of Fort Smith, NWT"

I took some of this from the School Counselling Programs Handbook (January 2004), but a lot of the information did not apply to Fort Smith, so I called up Marlene Evans and my elder Irene Sanderson, and they set me straight! My father, Jack Van Camp, shared what he knows about the bison and the wolves. Mahsi cho!

Duane Niatum, "Riding the Wake of the Paddle Journey"

Burien, Washington, Moon of Harvest, 1998, revised 2/2003

Laxaynam (1790–1885 or 1877) is the name of a revered chief and elder of our people, the Klallam (Jamestown band), during the early part of the nineteenth century. Sea Wolf is a guardian from a sacred narrative (myth) of the author's ancestors, which several tribes of the Pacific Northwest Coast have stories about. Takopid is the sacred mountain of the Puyallup. Whites call it Mount Rainier. Other Puget Sound tribes also have stories that celebrate the magic of this mountain, allude to it as an ancestor and power source.

About the Contributors

Judi Armbruster, a Karuk direct descendant, is one of the poets currently emerging from Indian country. Her poetry and unique digital art have been published internationally. One example is her poem "Meditation," which caps *The Book of Hope.* This volume was originally published in Iceland; it is dedicated to the victims of 9/11.

Lois Beardslee (Ojibwe/Lacandon) is the author of *Lies to Live By, Rachel's Children, Not Far Away,* and *The Women's Warrior Society.* Beardslee also preserves traditional Ojibwe art forms, including porcupine quillwork, sweetgrass basketry, and birch bark biting. She is an instructor in communications at Northwestern Michigan College.

Donna Beyer (née McCorrister) is a thirty-three-year-old Cree and Ojibway woman from Peguis First Nation, Manitoba, where she lived until the age of sixteen. It was in the university where Donna rediscovered a love for literature and writing, namely, Native literature. Donna is pursuing an MA in Native Literature at the University of Manitoba and reviving her maternal grandmother's language by learning Cree, with hopes of passing it on to her six-year-old daughter. She has also started a radio show in her home community, hoping to generate a greater awareness of and interest in Native literature.

Sherwin Bitsui is originally from White Cone, Arizona, on the Navajo Reservation. Currently, he lives in Tucson, Arizona. He is Diné of the Todich'ii'nii (Bitter Water Clan), born for the Tl'izilani (Many Goats Clan). He holds an AFA from the Institute of American Indian Arts Creative Writing Program and is currently completing his studies at the University of Arizona. He is the recipient of the 2000–2001 Individual Poet Grant from the Witter Bynner Foundation for Poetry, a 1999 Truman Capote Creative Writing Fellowship at IAIA, a Lannan Foundation Marfa Residency, and a 2006 Whiting Writers' Award. His books include *Shapeshift* (University of Arizona Press) and *Flood Song* (Copper Canyon).

Kim Blaeser (Anishinaabe), a professor at the University of Wisconsin–Milwaukee, is an enrolled member of the Minnesota Chippewa Tribe who grew up on the White Earth Reservation. Her publications include *Gerald Vizenor: Writing in the Oral Tradition* and collections of poetry: *Trailing You* (Native Writers' Circle of the Americas First Book Award), *Absentee Indians and Other Poems,* and *Apprenticed to Justice.* Blaeser's poetry, short fiction, essays, and critical works have also been widely anthologized. She is the editor of *Stories Migrating Home: A Collection of Anishinaabe Prose* and *Traces in Blood, Bone, and Stone: Contemporary Ojibwe Poetry.* Blaeser lives with her husband and two children in rural Lyons Township in Wisconsin.

Odilón Ramos Boza (Quichua) from Huancavelica, Peru, Instituto Superior Pedagógico Estatal de Huancavelica, is a Quechua professor of rural communities, currently in Pampachacra.

Joseph Bruchac lives with his wife, Carol, in the Adirondack mountain foothills town of Greenfield Center, New York, in the same house where his maternal grandparents raised him. Much of his writing draws on that land and his Abenaki ancestry. He and his two grown sons, James and Jesse, continue to work extensively in projects involving the understanding and preservation of the natural world, Abenaki culture, language (westernabenaki .com), and traditional Native skills. His poems, articles, and stories have appeared in over 500 publications, from *American Poetry Review* to *National Geographic.* He has authored more than 120 books for adults and children, and his honors include a Rockefeller Humanities fellowship, an NEA Writing Fellowship for Poetry, and the Lifetime Achievement Award from the Native Writers Circle of the Americas.

Jerry Brunoe is Wascopum. He was raised on the Warm Springs Reservation and is currently seeking a degree in Liberal Studies with a focus in writing at Oregon State University.

Tenille Campbell is a Dene author from English River First Nation. She has a creative writing diploma from St. Peter's College and a bachelor of arts from the University of Saskatchewan. She is currently working on her MFA in Creative Writing at the University of British Columbia. She is a fan of reading for fun, drinking coffee in large quantities, and scrapbooking.

Hilario Chacin is an Indigenous (Wayuu) bilingual poet who writes in Wayuunaiki and Castilian Spanish, born in La Guajira, Colombia, on

November 5, 1978. He has been a Cultural Director for the municipality of Paez, a specialist translator of the Ministro del Poder Popular para los Pueblos Indígenas (Ministry of Popular Power for Indigenous Peoples), Director for the Complejo Etnomédico y Cultural de La Guajira (Ethnomedical and Cultural Center of La Guajira), Historian for the municipality of Paez, and Municipal Coordinator for La Misión Cultura. Hilario Chacin has a bachelor's degree in Education and a master's degree in Anthropolinguistics from the Universidad de Zulia in Maracaibo, Venezuela. He teaches classes in Social Communication. Publications include *Lirica y narrativa desde una visión Wayuu* (A Wayuu View on Lyricism and Narrative); *Semantica y etnomedicina Wayuu* (Wayuu Semantics and Medicine); *Los hijos de la lluvia* (The Children of the Rain), a dual-language book of poetry written for children; and *Vestigios y memorias del Municipio Páez* (Vestiges and Memories of the Municipality of Paez).

Asani Charles, Choctaw, Chickasaw, and African American, begins her days with the ringing of a school bell. She teaches AP English Language and Literature in Dallas and enjoys teaching writing from a writer's perspective, further exploring the creative process. Asani recently recorded *Word Songs for Grandmas,* a collection of poems accompanied by Bear Claw Singers' Darrell Blackbear Sr. She calls it "poetry over powwow." After a lifetime in their native Southern California, Asani and family moved to Mesquite, Texas, where she spends her weekends listening to American Indian radio and hunting for local powwows to dance Women's Southern Cloth.

Rosa Chávez is a member of the Maya K'iche tribe on her father's side and the Maya Kaquiquel on her mother's side. She was born in Guatemala in 1980. In addition to being a poet, she's an actress and cultural committee member. Rosa Chávez has been invited to share her work at various literary events and festivals in Mexico, El Salvador, Costa Rica, Venezuela, Colombia, Chile, Peru, and Argentina. Publications include *Casa solitaria,* published in Guatemala in 2009; *PIEDRA,* published in Costa Rica in 2009; and *Los dos corazones de Elena Kame,* published in Argentina in 2009.

Fredy Romiero Campo Chicangana, poet of the Yanacona Community of Sur-Oriente of the Cauca, Colombia, and winner of the Nosside Unique Prix Global de Poesia, Italy, was born in 1964. His poems have been published by varied national magazines and newspapers. He has participated in festivals and conferences in Indigenous language and poetry in Mexico, Venezuela,

Chile, Ecuador, Colombia, the United States, and Peru. His work, in the Ancient Inca language of the Quechua, depicts Yanacona culture in *recovery of own language* and *songs of our people* and in *the ORALITURA in the indigenous cultures in Colombia*. He is a charter member of the Yanamauta group "knowledge and saberes yanaconas." Books include: *TAQUINAM CUYAYPA MANCHACHIPAK HUAÑUYMAN* (Songs of love to drive away the death), *ÑUKA YANACONA, SHIMI YUYAIPAS* (I Yanacona, word and memory), and *KINDE TUTAMANTA YARAVI NINA* (the colibrí at night undresses and other songs of the fire). He is a professor of cultural anthropology and former mayor of his pueblo.

Roberta Cordero (Chumash/Yaqui/Mestiza) was born in Santa Barbara, California, in 1942. Her maternal lineage is from León, Guanajuato, Mexico, and her paternal lineage is from Santa Barbara, California. As such, she was raised during the last vestiges of the Mestizo (i.e., mixed-blood of Indian and Spanish lineage) culture known as the Californio culture. Ms. Cordero grew up in Santa Barbara, where she attended grammar school and graduated from Bishop High School in 1960. She moved to Seattle, where she lived for thirty-five years and raised her five children. While there, she graduated cum laude and Phi Beta Kappa from the University of Washington School of Music as a voice major, and later from the University of Washington School of Law. Currently, she lives in her Chumash homeland and works as a professional peacemaker and conflict management specialist, training across the country in the areas of workplace change, interest-based communication, negotiation, mediation, cross-cultural effectiveness skills, and historic trauma. In addition, she is a cofounding board member of the Chumash Maritime Association, a nonprofit organization working to revitalize the maritime heritage of the Chumash people. She is blessed with six delightful grandchildren.

Jace DeCory (Lakota/Cheyenne River Sioux Tribe) has been an assistant professor with the American Indian Studies Program at Black Hills State University (instructor since January 1984), teaching in a variety of disciplines. Currently affiliated with the Department of History and Social Sciences, College of Arts and Sciences, Jace teaches primarily history and sociology courses. Jace's interests lie in Lakota history, art, philosophy, Indian women, and cultural change. Jace's guiding forces are her two sons, Sam Jr. and Dawson. She enjoys beading baby moccasins for relatives and friends. Jace credits the Lakota elders for providing guidance, prayers, and support throughout her life. Mitakuye Oyasin (For All My Relations).

Natalie Diaz (Mojave/Pima) was born and raised in the Fort Mojave Indian Village in Needles, California. After playing professional basketball in Europe and Asia for four years, she completed her MFA degree at Old Dominion University. She recently taught in a community college bridge program for Native high school students who want to attend college. She now lives on her reservation, working full-time on language reclamation with the four elders who are the only remaining fluent speakers of her language. Her work has been published or is forthcoming in the *Iowa Review, Prairie Schooner, Narrative, North American Review, Nimrod,* and others, and her first full volume, *When My Brother Was an Aztec,* is forthcoming from Copper Canyon Press.

Carolyn Dunn (Muskogee/Cherokee/Seminole) is a poet, playwright, musician, and mom living in Southern California. She has edited two books on American Indian literature and is the author of two books of poetry, including the award-winning *Outfoxing Coyote,* and a children's book, *Coyote Speaks.* A founding member of the all-women northern-style drum group The Mankillers, Dunn lives with her husband and children in the wilds of Indian Country, Los Angeles.

Heid E. Erdrich (Turtle Mountain Ojibwe) is the author of the poetry collections *The Mother's Tongue,* from Salt Press, and *Fishing for Myth,* from New Rivers Press. She coedited *Sister Nations: Native Women Writers on Community.* Her most recent poetry volume is *National Monuments,* from Michigan State University Press, winner of the Minnesota Book Award 2009. She cofounded Birchbark Books Press and the Turtle Mountain Writers Workshop. She is the curator at Ancient Traders Gallery in Minneapolis and is a wandering poet and teacher. Her home is in Minnesota.

Lise Erdrich (Turtle Mountain Ojibwe) was born in Minnesota, lives in Wahpeton, North Dakota, and has worked in Indian health and education for over twenty years. A graduate of the University of North Dakota and of Minnesota State University–Mankato, she is the author of the children's picture books *Sacagawea* and *Bears Make Rock Soup. Stories from Night Train,* her first book for adults (Coffee House Press), has received many awards, including the Minnesota Monthly Tamarack Award, the Many Mountains Moving Flash Fiction Contest, and Best of Show at the North Dakota State Fair, where "ZANIMOO" was exhibited between a pig and the pickles, jams, jellies, and preserves. Erdrich's work has appeared in several journals and anthologies, including *Sister Nations: Native American Women Writers on Community* and *Visit Teepee Town: Native Writings after the Detours.* Lise Erdrich offers a sharp-humored and powerful glimpse into rural communities and contemporary American Indian life and culture.

Louise Erdrich (Turtle Mountain Ojibwe) is the author of twelve novels, as well as volumes of poetry, children's books, and a memoir of early motherhood. Her debut novel, *Love Medicine,* won the National Book Critics Circle Award. *The Last Report on the Miracles at Little No Horse* was a finalist for the National Book Award. Her most recent novel, *The Plague of Doves,* is a *New York Times* best seller and winner of a Minnesota Book Award. Louise Erdrich lives in Minnesota with her daughters and is the owner of Birchbark Books, a small independent bookstore (www.birchbarkbooks.com).

Jennifer Elise Foerster is an alumna of the Institute of American Indian Arts in Santa Fe, New Mexico, and holds an MFA in writing from Vermont College. She has been the recipient of the Truman Capote Fellowship (IAIA), the Dorland Mountain Arts Colony Ataa'xum Fellowship, the Naropa Summer Writing Program Fellowship, the Vermont Studio Center Mill Atelier Fellowship, and a Stegner Fellowship at Stanford. She has been published in the literary journals *Red Ink Magazine, Tribal College Journal, Shenandoah, Atlantis, Cream City Review, Ploughshares,* and *Passages North.* Jennifer is a member of the Muscogee (Creek) Nation of Oklahoma and lives in San Francisco.

Jack D. Forbes (1934–2011) was Professor Emeritus and former Chair of Native American Studies at the University of California at Davis, where he served since 1969. He was of Powhatan-Renápe, Delaware-Lenápe, and other background. In 1960–61 he developed proposals for Native American Studies programs and for an Indigenous university. In 1971 the D-Q University came into being as a result of that proposal. He was also a poet, a writer of fiction, and a guest lecturer in Russia, Japan, Britain, the Netherlands, Germany, Italy, France, Canada, Belgium, Switzerland, Norway, Mexico, and elsewhere.

Santee Frazier is of the Oklahoma Cherokee people. He received his BFA from the Institute of American Indian Arts and his MFA from Syracuse University. *Dark Thirty* (University of Arizona Press) is his debut volume.

Diane Glancy (Cherokee) is Professor at Macalester College in St. Paul, Minnesota, where she has taught Native American Literature and Creative Writing. She currently is in a four-year sabbatical/early retirement program.

Her latest novel is *Stone Heart,* the story of Sacajawea, the young Shoshoni woman who traveled with Lewis and Clark. Recent books include *Rooms, New and Selected Poems* (Salt Publishers), *In-Between Places* (essays) (University of Arizona Press), and *The Dance Partner, Stories of the Ghost Dance* (Michigan State University Press).

Rain C. Goméz (L. Rain C. Goméz) is a poet, spoken word artist, academic, and musician currently attending the University of Oklahoma as a Sutton Doctoral Fellow. Her manuscript, *Smoked Mullet Cornbread Memory* (2009) won the First Book Award in poetry from the Native Writers' Circle of the Americas. Her poetry and critical work has appeared in various journals including past and upcoming issues of *Tidal Basin Review, River, Blood and Corn, Natural Bridge, American Indian Culture and Research Journal,* and *The Louisiana Folklife Journal.* She is the National Secretary of Wordcraft Circle of Native Writers and Storytellers, former Area Chair Native/Indigenous Studies Southwest/Texas PCA/ACA Annual Regional Conferences, and the newly appointed Editor-in-Chief of the Native Writers' Circle of the Americas Literary Digital Journal.

Reva "Mariah" S. Gover (Skidi-Pawnee and Tohono O'odham) currently lives and works in Tucson, Arizona. She is a single mother, who at the time of this writing is raising a fast-growing fourteen-year-old son. Mariah is close to completing her first novel, while continuing to create new and various pieces of poetry.

Joy Harjo was born in Tulsa, Oklahoma, and is a member of the Mvskoke Nation. Her seven books of poetry include *She Had Some Horses, The Woman Who Fell from the Sky,* and *How We Became Human: New and Selected Poems.* Awards include the New Mexico Governor's Award for Excellence in the Arts, the Lifetime Achievement Award from the Native Writers' Circle of the Americas, the William Carlos Williams Award from the Poetry Society of America, and a Rasmusson: U.S. Artists Fellowship. Her award-winning CDs include *Winding through the Milky Way* (NAMMY for Best Female Artist of the Year). She performs internationally with the Arrow Dynamics Band. Her one-woman show, *Wings of Night Sky, Wings of Morning Light,* premiered at the Wells Fargo Theater in 2009. She is a founding board member of the Native Arts and Cultures Foundation. Harjo writes a column, "Comings and Goings," for her tribal newspaper, the *Muscogee Nation News.* She lives in Albuquerque, New Mexico.

Allison Adelle Hedge Coke is descended from Huron, Cherokee, Creek, Métis, French Canadian, Lorraine, Portuguese, English, Scot, and Irish ascendants. Books include *Dog Road Woman* (American Book Award); *Off-Season City Pipe; Rock, Ghost, Willow, Deer; Blood Run*, and eight edited volumes. Performances include international poetry festivals in Colombia, Argentina, Venezuela, Jordan, and Canada. Hedge Coke came up working horses, tobacco, commercial fishing, in construction, and in factories. She mentors incarcerated youth and working-class writers, teaches writing as the Paul W. and Clarice Kingston Reynolds Chair, and is Associate Professor of Poetry and Writing at the University of Nebraska, Kearney.

Travis Hedge Coke lives and breathes in America. From mixed ethnicity, of complicated culture, he feels reluctant about mentioning either in bios, yet so compelled. Publications in *Many Mountains Moving, Mountain from the View, Dead Pretty Boys, Yellow Medicine Review, Birthmark Anthology (IAIA), Naropa Summer Magazine,* and *Gatherings (En'owkin Centre)*. He has read from New York City to Amman, Jordan. He currently coedits *Future Earth,* an online lit and arts journal, where he happily showcases all manner of great writers, artists, and musicians. Hedge Coke has an MFA from the University of California, Palm Desert. He teaches writing at the University of Nebraska, Kearney. Descent includes Huron, Choctaw, Cherokee, and Creek.

Gordon D. Henry, both poet and novelist, is an enrolled member of the White Earth Chippewa Tribe of Minnesota. An associate professor of English and American Studies at Michigan State University, he remains rooted in Mt. Pleasant, Michigan. Recently, he was appointed senior editor of the American Indian Studies Series at Michigan State University Press. His first novel, *The Light People,* won an American Book Award in 1995 and has recently been reissued from Michigan State University Press. Henry's poetry and fiction are anthologized in various collections, including *Songs from This Earth on Turtle's Back; Earth Song, Sky Spirit; Stories Migrating Home; Returning the Gift; Children of the Dragonfly;* and *Nothing But the Truth.* In 2004, Henry and George Cornell coauthored a middle-school text on the Ojibwe for Masoncrest Publishing. His poetry, fiction, and interviews have been translated and published in Spain, Italy, and Greece.

Jon Henson (Cheyenne) lives outside of Durango, Colorado, with his wife, Eliza, and two children. He is currently seeking a publisher for his most recent work, *Hanging out in the Afternoon.*

Lance Henson, born in Washington, D.C., in 1944, is Cheyenne, Oglala, and French. He was raised on a farm near Calumet, Oklahoma, by his great-aunt and great-uncle, Bertha and Bob Cook. He grew up living the Southern Cheyenne culture. He served in the U.S. Marine Corps after high school, during the Vietnam War, and is a graduate of Oklahoma College of Liberal Arts (now University of Science and Arts of Oklahoma) in Chickasha. He holds an MFA in creative writing from the University of Tulsa. Lance is a member of the Cheyenne Dog Soldier Society, the Native American Church, and the American Indian Movement (AIM). Lance has published seventeen books of poetry, half in the United States and half abroad. His poetry has been translated into twenty-five languages, and he has read and lectured in nine countries.

Roberta J. Hill, a poet of Wisconsin Oneida heritage, is the author of *Star Quilt,* a poetry collection that integrates her ancestral culture with European-based approaches to verse. Hill grew up in Wisconsin among the Oneida community and also in Green Bay; the family moved between the two locales several times. Hill has been a Loft Mentor, an instructor for the Poets-in-the-Schools Program, and a professor at the University of Wisconsin, Madison. She is a recently invited poet of the International Festival at Medellín.

Linda Hogan (Chickasaw) is an internationally recognized public speaker and author of poetry, fiction, and essays. Her most recent books are *Rounding the Human Corners* (Coffee House Press, 2008; a Pulitzer nominee) and *People of the Whale* (Norton, 2008). *Mean Spirit* was a winner of the Oklahoma Book Award and the Mountains and Plains Book Award, and a finalist for the Pulitzer. *Solar Storms* was a finalist for the International Impact Award. Other awards include finalist for the National Book Critics Circle Award, the Colorado Book Award, Minnesota State Arts Grant, an American Book Award, a Lannan Fellowship, a National Endowment for the Arts Fellowship, and a Guggenheim. Hogan has received the Lifetime Achievement Award from both the Native Writers Circle of the Americas and Wordcraft Circle. Professor Emerita of the University of Colorado, she is now the new Writer-in-Residence for the Chickasaw Nation and lives in Oklahoma.

LeAnne Howe (Choctaw) has served as the John and Renee Grisham Writer-in-Residence at the University of Mississippi, Oxford. She is the screenwriter for *Indian Country Diaries: Spiral of Fire,* a ninety-minute PBS documentary that aired nationally in November 2006. Howe is a professor at the University of Illinois, Urbana-Champaign, in the American Indian Studies program, English, and Theatre. Her first novel, *Shell Shaker* (Aunt Lute Books, San Francisco), received an American Book Award in 2002 from the Before Columbus Foundation. *Equinoxes rouges,* the French translation, was a 2004 finalist for the Prix Médicis Étranger, one of France's top literary awards. *Evidence of Red* (Salt Publishing) received the Oklahoma Book Award for Poetry in 2006. She publishes scholarly articles and fiction, plays, and poetry. Her second novel, *Miko Kings,* an Indian baseball story, is also from Aunt Lute Books. She is coediting *Seeing Red,* an anthology of reviews about American Indian films, due in 2012 from Michigan State University Press.

Al Hunter is the author of *Spirit Horses* and *The Recklessness of Love* (Kegedonce Press, 2001 and 2008, respectively). He was one of two writers invited from North America to attend the XVI Annual Festival Poesia de Medellín held in Medellín, Colombia, in 2006. Al is a citizen of the Anishinaabe Nation within Treaty 3. He is a proud member of the Caribou clan, whose roles and responsibilities include reconciliation, peacemaking, and the preservation of artistic, creative traditions of the Anishinaabeg. Al Hunter earned a BA from the College of St. Scholastica, Duluth, Minnesota, in 1997. His home is Rainy River First Nations, Ontario.

Hugo Jamioy is an internationally acclaimed poet-writer, native to the Indigenous group Camuentsa Cabeng Camentsá Biyá (Persons from Here with Authentic Knowledge and Language) in the Bengbe Uáman Tabanoc (Our Sacred Original Place) Municipality of Sibundoy, District of Putumayo, Colombia.

Joan Kane is Irish and Inupiaq Eskimo, with family from King Island and Mary's Igloo, Alaska. She earned her bachelor's degree from Harvard College and her MFA from Columbia University. Kane received the John Haines Award from Ice Floe Press in 2004, was a semifinalist for the Academy of American Poets' Walt Whitman Award in 2006, and received a 2007 individual artist award from the Rasmuson Foundation. In 2009 her play *The Gilded Tusk* won the Anchorage Musuem theater contest; she was selected as a finalist for the Poetry Foundation's Ruth Lilly Fellowship; and she received the Connie Boochever Fellowship from the Alaska State Council on the Arts, and a National Native Creative Development Program grant from the Longhouse

Education and Cultural Center. She is a 2009 Whiting Writers' Award winner. Along with her husband and son, she lives in Anchorage, Alaska.

Maurice Kenny, (Mohawk) recipient of the American Book Award, has authored *Tekonwatonti: Molly Brant, On Second Thought,* and *Backward to Forward* (essays); and *Tortured Skins and Other Fictions* and *In the Time of the Present* (poems), both from Michigan State University Press. He recently edited a collection of Native American short fiction, *Stories for a Winter's Night* (White Pine Press, 2000). The fall of 2003 saw his collection *Carving Hawk: New and Selected Poems* (White Pine Press). His latest poetry collections are *Connotations* and a new edition of *The Mama Poems,* which won the American Book Award some years ago. Kenny is Writer in Residence at SUNY Potsdam, recently was an invited speaker at the United Nations, and resides in Saranac Lake in the Adirondack Mountains.

Ariruma Kowii was born in Otavalo, Ecuador, August 4, 1961. Poet, professor, and editorialist of the Quitean newspaper *Hoy,* he belongs to the Quechua nation. He graduated in Social and Political Sciences from the Central University of Ecuador and teaches Literature and Studies about Culture in the Andean University Simón Bolívar in his country. He has published the poetry books *Mutsuktsurini* (1988), *Tsaitsik: Poemas para construir el futuro—edición bilingüe* (1993), and *Diccionario de nombres kichuas* (1998).

Jules Koostachin was born in Moose Factory and raised by her Cree-speaking grandparents for part of her childhood in Moosonee. She is Cree from Attawapiskat First Nations in Northern Ontario. Currently, she lives with her partner and four sons in Toronto and just completed her MFA in Documentary Media at Ryerson University. She has a number of published works, three produced short films, and two feature-length screenplays. Jules was a recipient of an *Ontario Arts Council Award* for developing one of her screenplays, which recently won for the Best Fresh Voice at the Female Eye Film Festival. Since childhood, her passion has been writing and continues to be so today.

Leonel Lienlaf, an Indigenous poet Mapuche, resides in Temuco, Chile, where he was born in 1971. For Leonel Lienlaf "the poetry is the feat and the feeling of its race, positions in its native language, mapudungún, that is to say, sung poetry." He has published, among other poetry books, *Has Awaked the Bird of My Heart* (1990). A world-renowned poet and activist, he is working with other activists on a campaign to protect Chile's native forests and the Indigenous peoples.

Chip Livingston is the author of the poetry collection *Museum of False Starts* (Gival Press) and the chapbook *Alarum*. His poems and stories have appeared widely, in *Columbia Poetry Review, Ploughshares, New American Writing,* and other journals. Chip descends from Muscogee Creek (Poarch Band), French Canadian, and Scottish ancestors. He divides his time between New York City, upstate Vermont, and Montevideo, Uruguay.

Layli Long Soldier is Oglala Lakota—her family is from Pine Ridge, South Dakota, and northwestern Idaho. She holds a BFA in Creative Writing from the Institute of American Indian Arts. She is a two-time recipient of the Truman Capote Creative Writing Fellowship. She is also a recipient of the 2009 Naropa University Poetry Scholarship. She has served as editor-in-chief for "Native Language Network" and other publications for the Indigenous Language Institute in Santa Fe, New Mexico. Her first chapbook of poetry is titled *Chromosomory* (Q Ave Press, 2009).

Lara Mann is a native of Kansas, an enrolled member of the Choctaw Nation of Oklahoma, and a University of Kansas alumna. She is of English, Irish, Choctaw, French, German, Scottish, Spanish, Cherokee, Welsh, and Mohawk descent. Mann received her master's of fine arts in Creative Writing in the spring of 2009, from the University of Illinois, Urbana-Champaign, and is anticipating the release of her first chapbook. Her work has been published in or is forthcoming from the *Connecticut Review, Many Mountains Moving,* and *Sentence Magazine,* among others

Lee Maracle is a member of the Sto:loh nation. She is the author of a number of books, including *Ravensong, Bent Box, Sojourner's Truth and Other Stories, Sundogs, Daughters Are Forever,* and *Will's Gardens*. She currently resides in Toronto and teaches at the University of Toronto and the Center for Indigenous Theatre.

Janet McAdams lives in Columbus, Ohio, teaches at Kenyon College, and edits the Earthworks Series of Indigenous Poetry for Salt Publishing. With Geary Hobson and Kathryn Walkiewicz, she is the coeditor of *The People Who Stayed: Southeastern Indian Writing after Removal* (University of Oklahoma Press, 2010). She grew up in Alabama and is descended from Scottish and Creek people. She is the author of two poetry collections, *The Island of Lost Luggage,* which won the Native Writers Circle of the Americas First Book Award and an American Book Award, and *Feral*. A novel, *Red Weather,* is under contract with the University of Arizona Press.

Brandy Nālani McDougall is Kanaka Maoli of Hawai'i, Maui, O'ahu, and Kaua'i lineages. A chapbook of her poetry is featured in *Effigies,* a Salt Indigenous anthology series edited by Allison Hedge Coke, and her first collection of poetry, *The Salt-Wind, Ka Makani Pa'akai,* was published by Kuleana 'Oiwi Press in 2008. A doctoral candidate in Hawaiian Literature, she currently teaches literature and creative writing at the Kamehameha Schools.

Molly McGlennen is mixed-blood (Anishinaabe, French, Irish), born and raised in Minneapolis, Minnesota. She presently teaches at Vassar, where she previously served as an Andrew W. Mellon Postdoctoral Fellow. She completed her PhD in Native American Studies from the University of California, Davis (2005), with her dissertation work on contemporary Native American women's poetry: "It Is Evidence of Faith to Create: Spirituality and Native American Women's Poetics." She also holds an MFA in Creative Writing from Mills College (1998). Her poetry is published in *Genocide of the Mind: New Native American Writing,* edited by MariJo Moore (Thunder's Mouth Press, 2003), and in special indigenous issues of *Shenandoah: The Washington and Lee University Review* and *Atlantis: A Women's Studies Journal.* Her first volume of poetry, *Like Fried Fish and Flour Biscuits,* was released by Salt Publishing in 2011.

Tiffany Midge is an enrolled Hunkpapa Lakota currently living in Moscow, Idaho, attending the University of Idaho's MFA in Poetry program. She has published *Outlaws, Renegades and Saints,* winner of the Diane Decorah Memorial Poetry Prize by the Native Writers Circle of the Americas, and *Guiding the Stars to Their Campfire, Driving the Salmon to Their Beds.*

Deborah A. Miranda is of Chumash/Esselen descent; her ancestors survived the Carmel and Santa Barbara missions. She is the author of *Indian Cartography* and *The Zen of La Llorona,* both poetry collections, and teaches Native American Literatures, Creative Writing, and Composition at Washington and Lee University. Currently she is at work on two writing projects, *Bad Indians: A Tribal Memoir* and *Written on the Bark of Trees: Praise Poems.* With her partner, poet Margo Solod, Deborah is grateful caretaker for sixty-eight acres of oak-and-cedar-rich land just outside Lexington, Virginia.

Paula Nelson is a member of the Eastern Band of Cherokee Indians located on the Qualla Boundary in Cherokee, North Carolina. She is a singer/songwriter and has been working on creating songs in the Cherokee language for children and families, to help with the Cherokee language revitalization efforts on the Qualla Boundary.

Duane Niatum has published six poetry books, most recently *The Crooked Beak of Love*. Another, *The Pull of the Green Kite,* is ready to publish. He has published several poems and stories in magazines and anthologies in the United States and Europe. He was three times nominated for a Pushcart Prize and is finishing his *Collected Poems*. Duane's writing is grounded in the Pacific Northwest landscape and its creatures, birds, animals, and plants, along with Klallam stories and characters, and is also influenced by the rich European culture of painting and writing. He is an enrolled member of the Klallam Tribe (Jamestown Band). He has a PhD in American Studies from the University of Michigan, Ann Arbor.

Margaret Noori received an MFA in Creative Writing and a PhD in English and Linguistics from the University of Minnesota. She is Director of the Comprehensive Studies Program and teaches the Anishinaabe Language and American Indian Literature at the University of Michigan. Her work primarily focuses on the recovery and maintenance of Anishinaabe language and literature. Current research interests include language proficiency and assessment, and the study of Indigenous literary aesthetics and rhetoric. For more information or to view current projects, visit www.ojibwe.net, where she and her colleague Howard Kimewon have created a space for language that is shared by academics and the Native community.

Jim Northrup (1) I was born on the Rez, live on the Rez, will probably die on the Rez. T'was a lot that happened in between, but it was just details. And from those details I make my stories. (2) I used to be known as a bullshitter, it is true. I know it is hard to believe, but it is true. But being a bullshitter didn't pay anything, so I decided to call myself a storyteller, a little better, more prestige. But it still didn't pay anything. I became a writer, a freelance writer. At first it was more free than lance, but eventually I started getting money for my words. When I became an author, a poet, a playwright, and a newspaper columnist, I could charge consultant's fees. Anishinaabe from the Fond du Lac Band of Lake Superior Chippewa.

dg nanouk okpik is Inupiaq, Inuit from Alaska. She is a graduate of Salish Kootenai College with an AFA in Liberal Arts, and a BFA in Creative Writing from the Institute of American Indian Arts, and will receive her MFA in Creative Writing/Poetry from Stonecoast College. Her work has been published in *Red Ink, Many Mountains Moving,* and *NYU Washington Square,* and has been featured in the Academy of American Poets fall 2009 issue of *American Poet,* by teacher Arthur Sze. Ms. okpik resides in Santa Fe, New Mexico, and is employed at Santa Fe Indian School. Her chapbook, *In The Time of Okvik,* was published in *Effigies* (Salt Publishing).

Sara Marie Ortiz is an Acoma Pueblo mixed-genre writer, filmmaker, and advocate. She is a graduate of the Institute of American Indian Arts (2006), where she earned a BFA in creative writing and received the Truman Capote Literary Fellowship. She has published widely, is a recent graduate of Antioch University Los Angeles, with an MFA in Creative Writing with a concentration in creative nonfiction (2009), and is currently working on her first full-length manuscript and a documentary on the life, work, and legacy of her father, Simon J. Ortiz.

Simon J. Ortiz, poet, fiction and creative nonfiction writer, and Professor at Arizona State University, is a member of the Acoma Pueblo Nation. He is author of *Woven Stone, Speaking for the Generations, After and Before the Lightning, Beyond the Reach of Time and Change, from Sand Creek, Out There Somewhere, The Good Rainbow Road, The People Shall Continue,* and other books. As a writer, teacher, and spokesperson, he insists Indigenous peoples must continuously struggle for the liberation and decolonization of their land, culture, and community.

Juanita Pahdopony is an Assistant Professor of Arts and Humanities at Comanche Nation College in Lawton, Oklahoma, and an enrolled member of Comanche Nation. She is active in the arts community and has exhibited her visual art in the American Indian Community House and also at the Museum of Arts and Design in New York City. She set a personal goal to use the Comanche language in writing and poetry as often as possible.

Elise Paschen (Osage) is the author of *Bestiary* (Red Hen Press, 2009), as well as *Infidelities,* winner of the Nicholas Roerich Poetry Prize, and *Houses: Coasts.* Her poems have been published in the *New Republic, Ploughshares,* and *Shenandoah,* among other magazines, and in numerous anthologies. She is coeditor of *Poetry in Motion, Poetry in Motion from Coast to Coast, Poetry Speaks,* and *Poetry Speaks Expanded,* and editor of *Poetry Speaks to Children* and *Poetry Speaks: Who I Am.* Former Executive Director of the Poetry Society of America, Paschen teaches in the MFA Writing Program at the School of the Art Institute of Chicago.

Jorge Miguel Cocom Pech (Mayan), born in Calkini, Campeche, Mexico, in 1952, is a poet, narrator, essayist, and professor in Maya language and Spanish. From 2002 to 2005, he was president of the Directive Council of Writers in Indigenous languages, A.C.: a national organization that gathers poets, narrators, playwrights, and essayists from Mexico. His book *Muk'ult'an in Nool, Grandpa's Secrets,* bilingual text Maya–Spanish, has been translated into French, Italian, Serbian, Romanian, and Arabic. He has participated in encounters, congresses, and festivals related to Indigenous cultures in Canada, the United States, Guatemala, Nicaragua, Panama, Colombia, Chile, and Venezuela.

Morela Del Valle Maneiro Poyo is a member of the Kariña tribe. Morela Maneiro won the first prize in the Bilingual Literature Contest *Kuai Nabaida—El Mar de Arriba—The Sea Above.* She shared first prize for unpublished work in the 23rd Annual International Poetry Contest, in Italy. Festivals include the International Poetry Festival of Medellín, Colombia; the International Book Fair in Havana, Cuba; the World Poetry Festival at Puerto Ordaz in Bolivar; the World Poetry Festival in Caracas, Venezuela; the international poetry conference Ritual de la Palabra, in Quito, Ecuador; the International Book Fair in Guayaquil, Ecuador; the 11th Annual International Book Fair of Caracas; and a Conference of the Indigenous Writers of America in Puerto Ayacucho, Venezuela.

Reale Redlance was born and is currently living in Edmonton, Alberta, as a student and writing creatively whenever inspired. He grew up away from the chaotic turmoils a family might impress on a young heart or mind and has found freedom; the expression of that freedom finds home within words, verses that seek a higher purpose. He will be attending the University of Alberta and is always ambitiously seeking new adventure wherever he roams, because he would rather live a life worth telling stories about, than live a life telling stories.

Marcie R. Rendon (White Earth Anishinabe) is a mother, grandmother, writer, and sometimes performance artist. Rendon was a 1998/99 recipient of the St. Paul Companies' LIN (Leadership in Neighborhoods) Award. Six of her plays were produced in the last eight years, with numerous one-acts, collaborations, and Raving Native productions also produced. Her poetry appears in numerous anthologies, her songs for choral pieces have been performed, and her second nonfiction children's book, *Farmer's Market: Families Working Together,* was published by CarolRhoda, Inc., in 2001.

Carter Revard, born and raised in Oklahoma on the Osage reservation, was given his Osage name in 1952. He earned a BA from the University of Tulsa, an MA at Oxford University on a Rhodes Scholarship, and then a PhD from Yale. A Gourd Dancer, he served on the Board of the American Indian Center in St. Louis. Awards include a 2005 Lifetime Achievement Award from the Native Writers Circle of the Americas; Writer of the Year from the Wordcraft Circle of Native Writers for his autobiography *Family Matters, Tribal Affairs;* and the Oklahoma Book Award in 1994 for *An Eagle Nation.* (In 2002, *Winning the Dust Bowl* was a finalist for that award.) He is Professor of English Emeritus at Washington University, St. Louis.

Cathy Tagnak Rexford, an Inupiaq of Barrow and Kaktovik, Alaska, was born in Anchorage, Alaska. She graduated from Evergreen State College with a bachelor of arts in Native American Studies in 2001. She graduated from the Institute of American Indian Arts with a bachelor of fine arts in Creative Writing in May 2006. She received a scholarship to attend the Idyllwild Arts Summer Poetry Workshop in 2005. She was a recipient of the Truman Capote Literary Scholarship for 2005–6 and attended the Summer Writing Program at Naropa University. Her work is rooted in her rich culture and the landscape of northern Alaska and has appeared in the 2005 Institute of American Indian Arts anthology *Fish Head Soup.* Her chapbook, titled *Black Ice,* was released in *Effigies* (Salt Publishing).

Gabriela Spears Rico is a Mexican Indian poet of P'urepecha and Matlatzinca ancestry. Gabriela was born in Michoacan, Mexico, and raised along the Central Coast of California. The daughter of a migrant farm worker, she followed the crops from Washington state to Oregon to California, learning to call labor camps and trailer parks home. After graduating from Stanford, she worked on prison reform in Washington, D.C., and participated in INCITE's Sisterfire! Cultural Arts Tour for Radical Women of Color. She was a recent participant in Mujeres Poetas en el País de las Nubes, an international women's poetry forum, which toured through the Mixtec region of Oaxaca, Mexico, and culminated in a performance at Mexico City's Palacio de Bellas Artes. She's currently a second-year doctoral student at U.C. Berkeley's program in Ethnic Studies, where she's interested in exploring how urban American Indian performance poetry functions as identity narrative for Native youth.

Michael Running Wolf Jr. is a member of the Northern Cheyenne Tribe in southeastern Montana. Currently, he is a graduate student in Computer Science at Montana State University.

Ralph Salisbury published three books in 2009: *Light from a Bullet Hole: Poems New and Selected, Blind Pumper at the Well* (poems), and *The Indian Who Bombed Berlin* (stories). He has received a *Northwest Review* Poetry Award, a Chapelbrook Award in poetry and fiction, and a Rockefeller Bellagio Award. He is of Cherokee descent.

Norys Odalia Saavedra Sanchez, born in Barquismeto, Lara, Venezuela, in 1972, is a poet and narrator. She received an Honorable Mention in the University Poetry Contest by Andrés Eloy Blanco. A member of Lara's association of writers and the national network of Venezuelan writers, she also created a Poetry in the Schools workshop in Holguin, Cuba, with the assistance of local writers. Member of a brigade for those fighting political battles, she is a champion of social welfare. She has written five books of poetry, among them *De Áridas Soledades* (2007), *Naranjos largos de viento,* and *Caza de animales en flor* (2009), and has been published in newspapers, magazines, and journals in Venezuela and throughout Latin America. She was recognized in a writers' discovery event in Alba. Her first book was noted on National Venezuelan Radio by the Mexican poet Pedro Martinez Escamilla and the poet of Santiago, Cuba, Reinaldo Garcia Blanco. Her work has appeared in the anthology *Un canto de Venezuela.* She participated in the Poesia en Movimiento (Exposición visual del metro de Caracas) in 2009.

Tessa Mychael Sayers is currently attending the University of Utah to obtain her master's degree in Educational Psychology. She is in the American Indian Teacher Training Program with plans to become a school counselor in a Native American tribal school. Poetry has been an interest of hers, especially poetry that reflects her personal feelings and experiences. She is a member of the Turtle Mountain band of Chippewa Indians.

M. L. Smoker is a member of the Ft. Peck Assiniboine and Sioux tribes in Montana. She recently published her first collection of poetry, *Another Attempt at Rescue,* with Hanging Loose Press. Currently, she works for the Indian Education Division of the Montana State Education Department.

Lindantonella Solano was born in Süchimma-Riohacha, La Guajira, Colombia, on January 7, in the year Wole Soyinka wrote *The Death of the King's Horseman*. Solano is a descendant of the clan Epiayu, educator of preschool, psychologist, a specialist in educational planning with emphasis in human development, a teacher of the University of the Guajira, a founding associate of the foundation Atrapasueños; and Director (principal) of Educaciónen's School of the Literary Creation. She works with the Workshops and Groups on Literary Creation of Talaüshi–Happiness. Her published books include *Kashi de 7 eneros desde el vientre de Süchiimma* (Editorial La Serpiente Emplumada, 2009).

James Thomas Stevens is a member of the Akwesasne Mohawk tribe in upstate New York. He attended the Institute of American Indian Arts, and the Jack Kerouac School of Disembodied Poetics at Naropa, and received his MFA from Brown University. Stevens is the author of *Tokinish* (First Intensity Press, 1994), *Combing the Snakes from His Hair* (Michigan State University Press, 2002), *(dis)Orient* (Palm Press, 2005), *Mohawk/Samoa: Transmigrations,* a collaborative book of poems with Samoan poet Caroline Sinavaiana (SubPress, 2006), *Bulle/Chimere* (First Intensity Press, 2006), and *A Bridge Dead in the Water* (Salt Publishing, 2007). He was Associate Professor in English and Director of American Indian Studies at the State University of New York College at Fredonia and is currently Professor of Poetry at the Institute of American Indian Arts. Stevens is a 2000 Whiting Writers' Award winner and a 2005 finalist for the National Poetry Series Award. He has done readings from Stirling, Scotland, to Grenoble, France, and Amman, Jordan, to Istanbul, Turkey.

Laura Tohe is Diné and the author/coeditor of five books of poetry: *Making Friends with Water; No Parole Today; Sister Nations: Native American Women Writers on Community; Dancing with the Wind;* and *Tseyi', Deep in the Rock*. She wrote a commissioned libretto, *Enemy Slayer,* for the Phoenix Symphony Orchestra, which premiered in Phoenix in 2008. She won the Arizona Book Association's Glyph Award for Best Book and Best Poetry for *Tseyi', Deep in the Rock* in 2007. She was a 2009 nominee for the Arizona Art Award. She teaches at Arizona State University.

Richard Van Camp is a proud member of the Dogrib (Tlicho) Nation from the Northwest Territories. He is the author of a novel, *The Lesser Blessed,* which will soon be a movie with First Generation Films; two children's books with Cree artist George Littlechild: *A Man Called Raven* and *What's the Most Beautiful Thing You Know about Horses?* and a collection of his short stories, *Angel Wing Splash Pattern.* He is also the author of the baby book *Welcome Song for Baby: A Lullaby for Newborns,* which was given to every newborn baby in British Columbia in 2008 through the Books for British Columbia Babies program. Richard's newest collection of short stories is *The Moon of Letting Go.*

Luke Warm Water is an enrolled Oglala Lakota who was born and raised in Rapid City, South Dakota. In 2005, he was awarded an Archibald Bush Foundation individual artist fellowship in poetry. Luke has won several poetry slams from Oregon to Germany. Recent magazine publication credits include *Indian Education Today* and *Red Ink.* Luke's latest book of poetry is *On Indian Time* (2005).

Orlando White is from Tólikan, Arizona. He is Diné (Navajo) of the Naaneesht'ézhi Tábaahí (Zuni Water's Edge Clan) and born for the Naakai Dine'e (Mexican Clan). He holds a BFA from the Institute of American Indian Arts and an MFA from Brown University. His poems have appeared in *Bombay Gin, Kenyon Review, Oregon Literary Review, Ploughshares, Salt Hill Journal, Sentence: A Journal of Prose Poetics, Talking Stick Native Arts Quarterly,* and elsewhere. He is a professor of writing at Diné College and lives in Tsaile, Arizona. *Bone Light* (Red Hen Press, 2009) is his first book.

Karenne Wood is an enrolled member of the Monacan Indian Nation and served on the Monacan Tribal Council for twelve years. She directs the Virginia Indian Heritage Program at the Virginia Foundation for the Humanities and is a PhD candidate and Ford Fellow in Anthropology at the University of Virginia, working to revitalize indigenous languages and cultural practices. She was previously the Repatriation Director for the Association on American Indian Affairs. She has worked at the National Museum of the American Indian as a researcher and directed a tribal history project with the Monacan Nation for six years. Wood held a gubernatorial appointment as Chair of the Virginia Council on Indians, and she served on the National Congress of American Indians' Repatriation Commission. Book include *Markings on Earth* (North American Native Authors Award for Poetry) and *The Virginia Indian Heritage Trail,* a guidebook now in its third edition. She holds an MFA in poetry from George Mason University.

Phil Young is of Cherokee and Scotch-Irish descent, born in Henryetta, Oklahoma, in 1947. As a member of the "Façade Buster Clan" (sorry, No Princesses!), his work affirms the necessity of "on/site for insight," geophysically/culturally/autobiographically. "Cultural raids" into tourist trading posts of the Southwest have become sources for performances, paintings, drawings, and mixed-media "Genuine Indian Burial sites." Satirical text accompanies the collected and fabricated items that unmask, subvert, and celebrate the demise of the "inauthentic–Genuine Indian," perpetuated in trading-post breeding grounds. Additional recent sources from the disabling effects of multiple sclerosis have entered the mixedbloodbodyscape. His awards include Millay Colony Residency, a Joan Mitchell Foundation Grant in Painting and Sculpture, and a New York Foundation for the Arts Fellowship in Sculpture. He is Professor of art at Hartwick College in Oneonta, New York. Young states that "the red clay of Oklahoma still runs in my veins."

Ofelia Zepeda is a Regents' Professor of Linguistics and recipient of the MacArthur Fellowship for her work in American Indian language education, maintenance, and recovery. Dr. Zepeda is a member of the Tohono O'odham Nation of southern Arizona, born and raised in Stanfield, Arizona. She is the series editor of Sun Tracks, a book series publishing Native American writers (University of Arizona Press). Ofelia Zepeda is one in a handful of Native authors writing and publishing in her first language. She currently has three books of poetry—*Ocean Power: Poems from the Desert, Jewed I-hoi/Earth Movements,* and *Where Clouds Are Formed*—and is the coeditor of *Home Places,* a celebration of twenty years of publications in the Sun Tracks series. Her poetry has also appeared in numerous anthologies and journals, including *Reinventing the Enemy's Language,* edited by Joy Harjo and Gloria Bird; *Fever Dreams,* edited by Leilani Wright and James Cervantes; *Poetry of the American West: A Columbia Anthology,* edited by Alison Deming; and *A Narrative Compass: Women's Writing Journeys,* edited by Betsy Hearne and Roberta S. Trite.

About the Translators

Irene Beibe was born in Buenos Aires, Argentina. Currently, she is an assistant professor at Muhlenberg College in Allentown, Pennsylvania. Her specialty is twentieth-century Spanish poetry. *Reflexiones y reflejos* is her debut book of poetry.

Gloria E. Chacón completed her PhD in literature at the University of California Santa Cruz. Chacón's research focuses on Indigenous literatures of Abya-Yala, Central American poetics and politics, and literary and cultural theories. She has written about Maya women's poetry and the emergence of Maya authors. Chacon is currently a CLIR postdoctoral fellow at the Charles Young Research Library.

John Damon (1951–2010) was a poet and professor in the English Department of the University of Nebraska at Kearney, who specialized as a linguist and medievalist. He was a scholar of Ofelia Zepeda's works and Tohono O'odham language.

Cristina Eisenberg is a writer and conservation biologist. She holds a master of arts degree in Environmental Writing from Prescott College and is completing her PhD in Forestry and Wildlife at Oregon State University, where she is a Boone and Crockett Conservation Fellow. Her first book, *The Wolf's Tooth: Keystone Predators, Trophic Cascades, and Biodiversity,* was published by Island Press in 2010. Her scientific research focuses on how wolves affect ecosystems. Eisenberg is Latina translator who also holds a BFA in painting and is a former newspaper and magazine columnist and editor, with essays in numerous journals and books. She and her family live in a log cabin in northwest Montana, in an area where the grizzly bear and wolf population outnumbers the human population.

Marisa Estelrich was born in Buenos Aires, Argentina. She moved to the United States in 1997, got her MA in Liberal Studies at Wake Forest

University, and is now finishing her MA in Spanish Language and Literature at the University of North Carolina in Greensboro. She is currently investigating the way in which testimonial forms evolved from responses to Southern Cone dictatorships to a dialogue of the subject/witness with other forms of violence, terror, and terrorism. She won the first prize at the III Certamen Internacional de Poesía y Narrativo Breve (Buenos Aires, 2003). Her first collection of short stories was published by Editorial Nuevoser (Buenos Aires, 2004).

Marleen Haboud is a UNESCO expert in endangered languages. She is currently the Director of the School of Linguistics and a professor and researcher at the Pontifical Catholic University of Ecuador, in Quito. Her main interests are contact linguistics, sociolinguistics, ethnolinguistics, bilingualism, and intercultural education. One of her main goals is to encourage the development of active documentation that would favor the reencountering and revitalization of indigenous languages of Ecuador.

Graciela Lucero-Hammer, a native of Córdoba, Argentina, is a translator of Latin American women writers, Associate Professor of Spanish, and Chair of the Modern Languages Department at Salem College, Winston-Salem, North Carolina.

Juan Felipe Herrera, a Native Californio Chicano poet, learned the art of writing and performance from living in a farm-worker family of storytellers, street theatres, the Iowa Writer's Workshop, and many mentors on the international and indigenous road. With twenty-eight books in various genres, his current work includes *Downtown Boy, Cinnamon Girl: Letters Found Inside a Cereal Box; 187 Reasons Mexicanos Can't Cross the Border* (PEN Award); and *Half the World in Light* (National Book Critics Circle Award). Juan Felipe Herrera teaches creative writing as the Tomás Rivera Endowed Chair, University of California, Riverside.

Laura Ortega is Mexican-American and bilingual in English and Spanish. Laura received her bachelor of arts in English: Writing from the University of Redlands, with emphasis in fiction. Laura is a recent graduate of the University of California–Riverside. Laura received her MFA in Creative Writing and Writing for the Performing Arts from the Palm Desert campus. Her thesis was a screenplay for a feature-length film, *Azahar.* Laura is the newest editor of *Future Earth Magazine,* which has opened her to edgy writing and edgier visual art.

Juan Nevarez is Latino and lives in Albuquerque, New Mexico.

Nicolás Suescún was born in Bogotá in 1937. A poet, translator, journalist, and bookseller with advanced secondary studies in Virginia, the University of Columbia, and the School of High Studies of Paris, upon his return to Bogotá, he was appointed Professor of English at the National University. He worked at the Buchholz bookstore, whose magazine *Echo* he directed, and founded the Extemporánea Bookstore. He was *diagramador* of the magazine *Nueva Frontera*. He has translated Rimbaud, Flaubert, Somerset Maugham, Ambrose Bierce, W. B. Yeats, Christopher Isherwood, and Stephen Crane. Works include *El retorno a casa, El último escalón, El extraño y otros cuentos, La vida es . . . , Los cadernos de N,* and *Oniromanía.*

Eugenia Toledo was born in Temuco, Chile. She came to the United States in 1975 to pursue degrees in Latin American and Spanish sixteenth-century literature. She is a poet and teaches writing workshops, writes literary articles, and creates book-objects combining words and graphic materials.

About the Cover Artist

Steven Yazzie was born in Newport Beach, California, and lives and works in Phoenix, Arizona. He is a visual artist working mostly in paint. He has taken part in numerous exhibitions, most notably at the Museum of Modern Art, New York; the National Museum of the American Indian, New York; the Art Gallery of Ontario; and the Museum of Contemporary Native Art, Santa Fe. For more information, visit www.stevenyazzie.com.

Source Credits

Unless otherwise indicated, the poems in this collection appear by permission of the authors.

τ¢ τ¢πος [To Topos]: Poetry International

The following poems and translations were included, or ran as versions thereof, in the Fall 2006/Winter 2007 edition of τ¢ τ¢πος: *Poetry International*, Oregon State University (*Ahani: Indigenous American Poetry*, guest edited by Allison Adelle Hedge Coke by invitation of Eric Wayne Dickey and Joseph Ohmann-Krause. The journal was founded by Roger Weaver. The assistant editor at the time of the edition was Genevieve Turner. © 2006 τ¢ τ¢πος Poetry Enterprises, is a 501(c)(3) Nonprofit Association, housed in the Department of Foreign Languages and Literatures, at Oregon State University, Corvallis, Oregon, 97331, USA. Joseph Ohmann-Krause and Eric Wayne Dickey remain the editors of the journal and press. *Ahani: Indigenous American Poetry*, ISSN 1091-6636, was supported in part by an Oregon Literary Fellowship to Publishers Grant and Amnesty International).

Judi Armbruster, "Living Rain," p. 229
Sherwin Bitsui, "Calyx," pp. 42–43; "Flood Song" (excerpt), p. 15
Odilón Ramos Boza, "Llama," "Llama," "A Poem to My Llama," pp. 208–9
Jerry Brunoe, "Love Poem #13: How Many Aubades Have Passed This Year Alone?"
    p. 255
Asani Charles, "Grease," p. 217
Roberta Cordero, "Bow-Riders," p. 232
Jace DeCory, "Sam, I Am," pp. 87–88
Rain C. Goméz, "Old Crawdad the Fisherman," p. 288
Jennifer Elise Foerster, "Leaving Tulsa," pp. 54–57
Jack D. Forbes, "Weenoway-Okaan," "Begging," "Naaga Elkee," "In a Little While,"
    "Opan," "Dawn," pp. 201–5
Santee Frazier, "Coin Laundry," pp. 218–19; "Cross-town," 221–22; "Nick Cheater,"
    p. 223
Reva "Mariah" S. Gover, "A Single Note," p. 109
Joy Harjo, "Eagle Song," p. 127

Allison Adelle Hedge Coke, "America, I Sing You Back," p. 327

Gordon D. Henry, "Simple Four Part Directions for Making Indian Lit," pp. 20–21; "Sonny's Wake 2000," p. 112

Jon Henson, "To Grow Older," p. 116; "By the River in Winter," p. 118

Lance Henson, "Poem from Amman," p. 210

LeAnne Howe, "The List We Make," p. 224–28

Al Hunter, "A Secret of Birds," "Lacuna," "Winter Birds," "Out of the Gallows," p. 128–31

Hugo Jamioy, "Aty Tima Zarkuney, At¨sbe Buiñent¨san Onÿnaná," p. 132; "Tima Aty Zarkuney, brote de mi sangre," p. 132; "Tima Aty Zarkuney, Flow of My Blood," p. 133; "Espej Ca Inÿna Yomn Ndegombr Soy," p. 133; "Plateada es la realidad," p. 134; "Silvery Is Reality," p. 134; "Shinÿ y juashcón," p. 144; "Eclipse," p. 144; "Eclipse," p. 145; "Shecuat¨sëng Bet¨sa¨soc," p. 152; "Los Pies En La Cabeza," p. 152; "The Feet on the Head," p. 152; "Tonday chiatayán, nÿe sënjenojuabó," p. 146; "No dije nada, solo pensé," p. 146; "I Did Not Say Anything, Just Thought," p. 147

Ariruma Kowii, "Vivitaman," p. 157; "A, Virginia," p. 158; "Life," pp. 159–60; "Shamukpacha Wañukrinmi," pp. 161–62; "El Mañana Está en Peligro," pp. 162–63; "Tomorrow Is in Danger," pp. 164–65; "Pachaka," p. 166; "El Tiempo," p. 166–67; "Time," p. 167; "May Sumak Kayman," p. 177; "Canto a la Dignidad," p. 178; "A Song to Dignity," p. 179

Leonel Lienlaf, "Bajan Gritando Ellos Sobre los Campos," p. 192; "Bajan Gritando Ellos Sobre los Campos," p. 193; "They Come Down Yelling Through the Fields," p. 194; "Palabras Dichas," p. 197; "Palabras Dichas," p. 197; "Palabras Dichas," p. 197; "Lluvia," p. 198; "Lluvia," p. 198; "Lluvia" p. 198

Brandy Nālani McDougall, "Hāloa Naka," "The History of This Place," pp. 49–50

Molly McGlennen, "Interwoven," p. 86

Tiffany Midge, "Stories Are Alive Beings," "At the Fish Ladder," "Oil Spill," "Abstraction," pp. 62–64

Deborah A. Miranda, "Credo," "Ishi at Large," pp. 64–66

Paula Nelson, "A-ni-no-gi-i De-s-gv-i," "Trees Are Singing," "Land Song (from the hearts of the elders)," "Land Song (from the hearts of the elders)," pp. 206–7

dg nanouk okpik, "Sinnaktuq (Dream)," pp. 69–79; "On Poetics," pp. 71–72

Juanita Pahdopony, "Taa Nʉmʉ Tekwa Hʉrʉunʉ," "The Loss of Our Language," p. 205

Jorge Miguel Cocom Pech, "Fragmentos del Libro Inédito: El Chilam Balam de Calkiní," "Fragmentos del Libro Inédito: El Chilam Balam de Calkiní," "Fragments from the unedited book: The Chilam Balam of Calkini," "El niño maestro," "The Kid Teacher," pp. 186–91

Marcie R. Rendon, "My Child's Hunger...," "Foster Care Blues Cont.," "Security," pp. 295–97

Cathy Tagnak Rexford, "The Ecology of Subsistence," "Baleen Scrimshaw as 16 mm Film," pp. 35–36

Gabriela Erandi Rico, "Eulogy for Ramona," "Strawberry Hands," pp. 304–8

Michael Running Wolf Jr., "I Chased You," p. 249

Tessa Mychael Sayers, "New Lessons" (photograph by Chad Braithwaite), p. 237

M. L. Smoker, "Equilibrium," p. 73; "Back Again," p. 75

James Thomas Stevens, "Isère," pp. 31–32

Orlando White, "Ars Poetica," "Ats'íísts'in," pp. 76–78

Phil Young, "Wetumka Is a Mythic Place," "Wetumka II," pp. 256–59

Other Publications

Sherwin Bitsui, "Flood Song" (revised excerpt), in *Flood Song,* © 2009 (Port Townsend: Copper Canyon Press).

Fredy Romeiro Campo Chicangana, "Espíritu De Grulla y Espíritu Quechua," and "Crane Spirit and Quechua Spirit," "Danza de Amor," "Dance of Love" 32.1 (Winter 2010/2011), *Platte Valley Review,* http://www.plattevalleyreview.org/Webpages/Author%20Pages/A-K/Chicangana.html.

Heid Erdrich, "Liminal" and "ebay bones," in *National Monuments,* © 2008 (East Lansing: Michigan State University Press).

Santee Frazier, "Coin Laundry," "Cross-Town," "Nick Cheater," in *Dark Thirty,* © 2009 by Santee Frazier (Tucson: University of Arizona Press), pp. 218–19, 221–23.

Allison Hedge Coke, "America, I Sing You Back," originally presented at Memorias, 2005, Poetry of the International Poetry Festival of Medellín, Colombia; "Platte Mares," 12.3 (July/August/September 2009) *Talking Stick: Native Arts Quarterly,* http://www.amerinda.org/newsletter/12-3/hedgecoke.html#1.

Travis Hedge Coke, "Impromptu 49er, 1:25 a.m. in Los Angeles," first ran in *River-babble,* 2011.

Linda Hogan, "First Language" and "The Sandhills," *Platte Valley Review* 32.1 (Winter 2010/2011), http://www.plattevalleyreview.org/Webpages/Author%20Pages/A-K/Hogan.html.

Joan Kane, "Syllabics," 14.2 (April/May/June 2011) *Talking Stick: Native Arts Quarterly* (New York, New York: AmerInd).

Layli Long Soldier, "Burial Flight," in *Chromosomory,* © 2010 (Q Ave Press), www.qavepress.com.

Brandy Nālani McDougall, "Hāloa Naka" and "The History of This Place," in *Return to the Kula House,* chapbook published in *Effigies,* A. A. Hedge Coke, editor, June 2009 (Cambridge: Salt Publishing).

dg nanouk okpik, "Sinnaktuq (Dream)," in *In the time of Okvik,* chapbook published in *Effigies,* A. A. Hedge Coke, editor, June 2009 (Cambridge: Salt Publishing).

Simon Ortiz, "1.," "2.," "3.," and "4." from *Spiral Lands/Chapter 3*, text by Simon J. Ortiz, photographs by Andrea Geyer, http://www.andreageyer.info/projects/ spiral_lands/spiral_lands_3/SpiralPages/spiral.html.

Elise Paschen, "Magnificent Frigatebird," "Barn Owl and Moon," and "Wí'-gi-e," in *Bestiary,* © 2009 (Granada Hills, CA: Red Hen Press).

Cathy Tagnak Rexford, "The Ecology of Subsistence," and "Baleen Scrimshaw as 16 mm Film," in *Black Ice,* chapbook published in *Effigies,* A. A. Hedge Coke, editor, June 2009 (Cambridge: Salt Publishing).

Orlando White, "Ars Poetica" and "Ats'íists'in," in *Bone Light,* A. A. Hedge Coke, series editor, © 2009 (Los Angeles: Red Hen Press).

Ofelia Zepeda, "Ñeñe'i Ha-ṣa:gid," "In the Midst of Songs," in *Where Clouds Are Formed,* © 2008 by Ofelia Zepeda (Tucson: University of Arizona Press), pp. 28, 29.

Ofelia Zepeda, "Jeweḍ 'I-hoi," "Earth Movement," reprinted here with permission from the publisher. This poem and translation first appeared in *Jeweḍ 'I-hoi/Earth Movement,* © 1997 (Tucson: Kore Press).

Ofelia Zepeda, "Okokoi," "Mourning Dove," reprinted here with permission from the publisher. This poem and translation first appeared in *Mourning Dove,* © 2005 (Tucson: Kore Press Broadside).